MW01089687

Copyright © 2001 Nick Bollow, Rita Berg, & Marya Tyler
Cover Art & Illustrations by David Ramey

ISBN 1-882664-71-X

All rights reserved. The publisher grants the original purchaser of this book the right to reprint por-
tions of the book for classroom use. Otherwise, no part of this book may be reproduced in any
form, except for brief reviews, without written permission of the publisher.

PRUFROCK PRESS, INC.
P.O. Box 8813
Waco, TX 76714-8813
Phone: (800) 998-2208
Fax: (800) 240-0333
www.prufrock.com

Contents

Contents Continued

Foreword

Why *Alien Math*?

This book is the end result of what can happen when inquisitive minds are challenged and left unbridled on a single assignment. Mrs. Tyler gave her sixth grade gifted math students, one of whom was Nick Bollow, an assignment to convert base 6 numbers to base 10 and vice versa. Mrs. Berg, who had been invited by Mrs. Tyler to present a probability unit, was considering their base 6 assignment and was curious if base 6 numbers could be added without converting to base 10. These remarkable students were always eager to tackle any challenge they were given, and within a few minutes, they were adding in base 6. What was the next logical step? If addition was possible in base 6, then surely subtraction was possible as well. Of course it was! Okay, what about multiplication? Well, that took a little longer, but still that was no problem for these students. They even discovered some interesting patterns in the base 6 multiplication tables. Voila! One-third of the material for *Alien Math* was born!

Armed only with their knowledge of addition, subtraction, multiplication, and division in their own base 10, these students were able to apply the known to the unknown, the familiar to the unfamiliar. Since this method of problem solving is so invaluable, why not write a book guiding other teachers and students through a similar problem-solving process?

Our base 10 has been adopted because we have 10 fingers. Some ancient civilizations used base 20 because they counted toes as well as fingers. Imagine a world where the number of fingers or appendages was other than 10. In all likelihood, the base for numbers in that world would be entirely different. Thus arises the premise for *Alien Math*.

The authors would like to thank Derek Blanchard, Shea Chyou, Stefanie Schwecke, and Terese Gierach, the other four students of that gifted math class whose love for learning inspired us to write this book.

Why a Book About Number Bases?

Looking beyond our base 10 system (based on 10 numerals, 0, 1, 2, 3, 4, 5, 6, 7, 8, and 9) is a mind-expanding, consciousness-raising experience.

Okay, it's mind-expanding. But is it relevant?

Sure! Not every culture has always used our base 10 system.
- The Mayans of Central America used a base 5 counting system.
- The Gaelic people of ancient France used a base 20 counting system.
- The Sumerians and Babylonians used base 60.

But what about today? Is it still useful today?

- The San people of Africa *still* use a modified binary counting system and count, "one, one pair, one pair and one, two pairs, two pairs and one, three pairs, three pairs and one ..."
- Other present-day tribal peoples such as the Zamuco Indians of South America, the Parb people of New Guinea, and the Kauralgal people of Australia also use binary systems.

But how will learning about this be useful to me?

- The binary counting system is the **number system of the new millennium**! Computers read only "electricity on" and "electricity off." Give a computer a number like 100101 and the computer reads: On, Off, Off, On, Off, On. It's as easy as that. So you see, zero and one are the basis of every computer function. Groups of these numbers are stored using the hexadecimal system. You'll learn about that later in *Alien Math*.

But do aliens really exist?

Does Alien Math Support the NCTM Standards?

Alien Math wholeheartedly supports the standards formulated and updated by the National Council of Teacher of Mathematics. As the NCTM guidelines suggest, this book:

- centers first and foremost on **problem solving**;
- offers new understanding of systems of mathematical **communication**;
- builds understanding in the use of deductive and inductive **reasoning**;
- **connects mathematics** with science and language arts;
- provides a heightened **number sense**, recognizing equivalent forms;
- leads students to develop and apply **number theory concepts**;
- provides plenty of practice in **computation** and **estimation**; and
- uses **tables** to discover patterns and functions.

An exploration of number bases outside your own is the purest, surest path to a clear understanding of our own number system.

Alien Math is arranged to allow for discovery! This is not a rote, do-it-this-way-and-don't-ask-why textbook. It's not even a do-it-this-way-and-we'll-show-you-why textbook. *Alien Math* is a discovery book, and your students will thank you for allowing them to scout their own way through the mountains of mathematics, assisted by you as a guide only when the way seems unclear.

How To Use This Book

This book has been divided into two parts:
(1) Starlogs with Answer Key; and
(2) Space Traveler's Training Manual with Space Traveler's Training Manual Answer Key.

Starlogs

The Starlogs must be used in order to provide continuity to the story and to help the students learn the material.

Note the different fonts and subscripts in the Starlogs. The number system of the individual thinking or speaking is identified by the font. The fonts and who they represent are evident, but are shown below:

- Space Traveler
- Mr. Alien (Base 6)
- **The Binarians (Base 2)**
- The Hexadecimites (Base 16)

Never fear, the Answer Key is here! It is recommended that the teacher read the answer key and detailed explanations before guiding the discovery learning. If a certain Starlog seems too difficult, please try it anyway. It is absolutely amazing what gifted math students can grasp.

Space Traveler's Training Manual

Homework assignments are offered in the Space Traveler's Training Manual. Each Starlog has its own corresponding Training Manual. "Above and Beyond" extends beyond into higher level thinking for high-ability students.

Just passed the Andromeda Galaxy and I'm losing fuel at an astounding rate. No choice but to land on that uncharted planet—if I'm lucky.

Here goes … fasten hatches … rework configurations … contact starbase … fasten harness … (undo harness, use restroom) … redo harness … prepare to crash …

Where am I? Now I remember. The crash! Amazingly, my space scooter and I appear to be OK.

I am being approached! It has some humanoid characteristics—two hands, but interesting—only three fingers on each hand.

"Your arrival is fortuitous."

Hey, it spoke! I don't see any mouth. English of all things! It must have read my mind ...

"Good. You learn quickly. We have been awaiting your arrival expectantly. It is unfortunate that we had to puncture your fuel tank, but necessary. We are sure you will ultimately understand."

So how do I communicate with this guy? I decide to talk. "Well, now that you've shot down my ship, are you going to eat me or are you going to help me?"

"That depends upon your actions. We have long been interested in other forms of life and wish to determine if your species is among those we classify as intelligent.

To this end, we have arranged for a number of challenges. You will need to meet these challenges If you do, you will acquire the parts to repair your space-scooter and you will be able to return to your planet. Furthermore, your species shall merit classification as intelligent."

"What happens if I don't?"

"Species that do not possess classification as intelligent do not receive representation in the Galactic Council."

"So?"

"The Galactic Council determines, among other things, where hyperspace traffic lanes are placed. Your planet happens to be in the way of a proposed traffic lane. You understand?"

Gulp.

STARLOG 1400

I have received Phase I of my challenge. They have instructed me to catch and collect 100 oogles. What are oogles?

"Oogles are small creatures. They are unmistakably cylindrical, usually no longer than one of your hands, and have no noticeable appendages. You might find their ecological niche similar to that of your rodents. Your task, as stated before, is to collect 100 within 10 minutes."

Chased varmints for six minutes, and I've only collected 36. The guy, I'll call him Mr. Alien, didn't mention these critters stink, or the fact that they leave droppings everywhere. Oh, no! Mr. Alien is coming back early, and I'm not done!

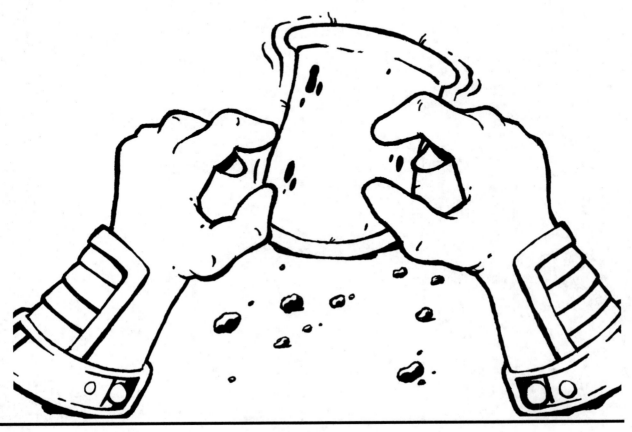

"You have completed phase one."

I have only 36 oogles. He distinctly asked for 100. He thinks I have 100 oogles? Oh well, if he doesn't notice I won't say a word.

"You have indeed accomplished the task, and I am not early. The second phase of your challenge is to determine why I was on time … and why you have enough."

Oh great! What does he mean? How can 10 minutes be 6 minutes? Mr. Alien waves good-bye with a cocky grin on his face (if you can call it a face). Wait a minute! He has three fingers on each of two hands—maybe their number system is based on 6 digits!

He said 10 minutes, but he was back in 6 minutes. I bet that's it! When we count we call the last finger 10. Their last finger they call 10, but their 10 must mean 6. Makes sense.

Is that why I had enough oogles? Does 36 in our base 10 system mean the same thing as 100 in their system?

Let's see, they have only six numbers: 0, 1, 2, 3, 4, and 5. Six numbers, base 6.

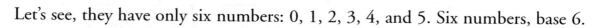

How do I count in base 6?					
$1 = 1_6$	$7 = 11_6$	13 =	19 =	25 =	31 =
$2 = 2_6$	$8 = 12_6$	14 =	20 =	26 =	32 =
$3 = 3_6$	9 =	15 =	21 =	27 =	33 =
$4 = 4_6$	10 =	16 =	22 =	28 =	34 =
$5 = 5_6$	11 =	17 =	23 =	29 =	35 =
$6 = 10_6$	12 =	18 =	24 =	30 =	36 =

It works! Let me see if I can get the hang of this. Back home, we have the one's place, the ten's place, and the hundred's place. Each one is a power of 10: 10^0, 10^1, and 10^2. Is the same thing true for base 6, only powers of 6?

If Mr. Alien says 10, what does that mean to me? 10_6 = _____ $_{10}$

If he says 100? 100_6 = _____ $_{10}$

If he says 1000? 1000_6 = _____ $_{10}$

If he says 10000? 10000_6 = _____ $_{10}$

Looks like I'm going to have to learn to think in base 6. I need to practice counting. How about oogle droppings? There are 72 on my shoes alone. Now what is 72 in base 6?

72_{10} = _____ $_6$?

There are also at least 55 oogle droppings in my shoes. Yuck.

55_{10} = _____ $_6$?

And I pick another 113 oogle droppings out of my pockets, cuffs, and hair.

113_{10} = _____ $_6$?

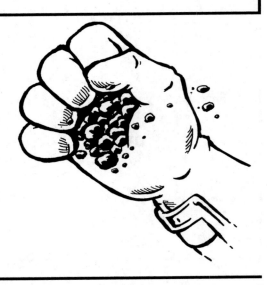

I got restless waiting for Mr. Alien to return, so I went exploring. I've been following this road for 30 minutes (50 minutes in base 6. Hey! I'm getting good!), and it looks like I'm coming to a town. Other than the fact that the houses look like giant orange meatballs, I see some similarities to Earth.

Look at this sign ... weird. Wow! It changed to English while I looked at it. Signs that read your mind! This place is incredible. You know, it could be a population sign, because when I passed it, it added 1. Hey, when I go back out, it takes 1 away! Fantastic! The population, including me, is 1435. Of course, that's base 6. What would it be in base 10?

$$1435_6 = \underline{\hspace{1cm}}_{10}$$

Looks like a swimming pool ahead. It appears to be filled with pink slime and clear jelly beans, but it does look like a swimming pool. Let's see, the sign says, "Maximum Capacity = 432." Hmm ...

$$432_6 = \underline{\hspace{1cm}}_{10}$$

Okay, I'm hungry. The sign says "Corgle Broil Tonight." A restaurant? Something edible? I'll soon find out.

"May I help you, sir?" An important-looking figure approaches. "You may need this," he says and he (at least I think it's a he) offers me a menu.

Menu

Item	Price
Horndabber with Rotsa	33 roogegs
Glooglib	14 roogegs
Hinkledamper	42 roogegs
Corgle	125 roogegs
Zoople	152 roogegs
Koojee	51 roogegs
Porveq	44 roogegs
Handerschnap	131 roogegs
with Moorgley	202 roogegs

Roogegs are the universal space dollars. Good.

How much does each dish cost in base 10?

Horndabber with Rotsa	33_6 roogegs = _____$_{10}$
Glooglib	14_6 roogegs = _____$_{10}$
Hinkledamper	42_6 roogegs = _____$_{10}$
Corgle	125_6 roogegs = _____$_{10}$
Zoople	152_6 roogegs = _____$_{10}$
Koojee	51_6 roogegs = _____$_{10}$
Porveq	44_6 roogegs = _____$_{10}$
Handerschnap	131_6 roogegs = _____$_{10}$
with Moorgley	202_6 roogegs = _____$_{10}$

Not knowing what any of these things are, I close my eyes and point. I order the glooglib. A few minutes later, he/she/it lays down a batch of what must be glooglib in front of me and then leaves. Unfortunately, the glooglib is still moving. They crawl across the napkin and are headed down the table leg when the waiter sees my distress and scoops them up. He asks me if I enjoyed my meal. "Fine, thank you." (I'm trying to be nice. It's hard even having to think nice here, because they can read my mind.)

"Maybe I'll try the horndabber with rotsa."

Something tells me I made a mistake. He brings a plate of aluminum foil scraps—greasy, aluminum foil scraps. What a waste of good money. I tell him I can't eat this.

"You might like the handerschnap with moorgley."

Can it be? It looks a lot like a cheese pizza! It looks delightful. I'm getting ready to dig in when the waiter brings out a dish and begins to sprinkle the pizza with what I am sure are oogle droppings. I tell him to please stop.

"But these are the moorgley you ordered."

"No moorgley! I've changed my mind." I cautiously eat the handerschnap and ask for my bill.

How much do I owe for the glooglib, horndabber with rotsa, and the handerschnap? (He didn't charge me for the moorgley.)

_____ roogegs for the glooglib
_____ roogegs for the horndabber with rotsa
_____ roogegs for the handerschnap

_____ **Total cost in roogegs**

I put 100_{10} roogegs on the table and leave.

$$\underline{100}_{10} \quad \text{roogegs}$$
$$\underline{-}_{10} \quad \text{total cost in roogegs}$$
$$\underline{}_{10} \quad \text{change in roogegs}$$

I left a tip of _____$_{6}$ **roogegs. I hope it's enough.**

I realize I can't afford to keep eating in restaurants, even though I have a few galactic travelers' cheques. I head over to what looks like a grocery store, take a hover-cart, and zoom around the aisles. Nothing edible here. Wait! I see something that looks like cookies. They smell like Dad's socks, but I can't be too picky. The cookies cost 3 roogegs per box. I select two boxes.

_____$_6$ roogegs for the 1st box of sock cookies
_____$_6$ roogegs for the 2nd box of sock cookies
_____$_6$ **Total cost for 2 boxes of sock cookies**

Hey now! An exotic food section! Maybe there is some Earth food! Yes! Unfortunately, all I see are jars of pickled pig feet. I'll take what I can get. One jar for 25_6 roogegs

_____$_6$ roogegs for the 2 boxes of sock cookies
_____$_6$ roogegs for the pig feet
_____$_6$ **Total cost so far**

Wait! Unbelievable! Chocolate ice cream for sale! These creatures have some taste after all. One gallon costs 10_6 roogegs. I buy 5 gallons (even Mom would understand).

_____$_6$ roogegs for sock cookies and pig feet

_____$_6$ roogegs for 5 gallons of chocolate ice cream

_____$_6$ **Total cost for everything**

There's no check-out, just an automatic scanner in the cart. It looks like I must drop the roogegs in this spiral vacuum tube. Darn, my travelers' cheques are all in 100_{10} roogeg notes. It better give me change!

100_{10} roogegs _____$_6$ roogegs

minus _____$_6$ total cost

---

equals _____$_6$ **change in roogegs**

It does.

A spoonful of chocolatey goodness. Feels like heaven. I'll be so glad to go home and be done with this aluminum foil and base 6 stuff.

I suddenly find myself transported back to the star-scooter, and I am now covered with 5 gallons of melted, sticky, chocolate ice cream. Mr. Alien peers down from above.

"My ice cream!"

"It liquefied during the exlocation. You are tired of using base 6?"

He could even read my mind long distance?

"How difficult it must be for you trapped within your own mind. It's now time for Phase III of your challenge. You will need liquid plutonium fuel for your space-scooter. Of course, plutonium fuel is so primitive, you won't find any here. I'm sending you to the Binarians. There you will also fill out a survey, which you should find less invasive than the usual dissection. Be sure to exercise caution."

"Binarians? Dissection?"

I find myself sitting on top of water in the middle of a lake. Here comes a Binarian. I wonder if they can read my mind. I better watch what I think.

"Expend zero effort. We know what you are going to think. This is true."

Gulp. Aliens with two heads. What next?

"Allow us to introduce ourselves. I'm Zero and this is One."

Each head has a name? Interesting. "I'm here to …"

"… get some plutonium fuel. This is true," said Zero.

Now the other head talks.

"You shall take this vacuum tube to the subterranean hover module. Wait for the 1010th stop to disembark. More directions will be given to you there."

"Okay, thanks. See you two later." They look at me strangely.

"Two? This is a false term," they respond in confused unison.

I'm thinking about why Zero and One aren't familiar with "two" when I am sucked into the vacuum tube and down into what must be the subterranean hover module. Their instruction was to wait through 1010 stops. This is going to take forever.

Somebody left a newspaper, but I can't read it. It's just a bunch of indiscernible doodles. Oh, one page is all numbers. But check this out, they are all 1's and 0's. Not a single 2, 3, or any other number. It's been a half-hour; only 6 stops have gone by. There goes stop number 7. No one gets off.

Why didn't Zero-One know what "two" meant? Even Mr. Alien knew the meaning of "two." Wait a minute, Zero-One doesn't have any arms. No fingers—the Binarians probably count by 2s instead of 10s like us or 6s like the Hexadotes. That makes sense considering they have two heads.

This is stop number 8. A bunch of Binarians get off; some more get on.

So if they only have two numbers, 0 and 1, then 2_{10} = _____$_2$?

This is stop number 9.

I had better learn to count in Binarian.

$0 = \rule{1.5em}{0.4pt}_2$ $1 = \rule{1.5em}{0.4pt}_2$ $2 = \rule{1.5em}{0.4pt}_2$ $3 = \rule{1.5em}{0.4pt}_2$ $4 = \rule{1.5em}{0.4pt}_2$

$5 = \rule{1.5em}{0.4pt}_2$ $6 = \rule{1.5em}{0.4pt}_2$ $7 = \rule{1.5em}{0.4pt}_2$ $8 = \rule{1.5em}{0.4pt}_2$ $9 = \rule{1.5em}{0.4pt}_2$

Tenth stop.

Do I get off here or not?

$1010_2 = \rule{6em}{0.4pt}_{10}$

That was close. Almost missed my stop. Now what? They said I'd get more instructions here. Here I am, light years from home, lost in a subterranean hover module station on a planet where they give you aluminum foil to eat, and if I mess up, Earth will be obliterated to put in a hyperspace traffic lane. Not only that, my ice cream melted.

"Patience," a voice emanates from nowhere as an orange glow envelops me. **"We cannot communicate with a restless mind."**

I calm myself.

"The plutonium you seek is 100000 steps up. You may begin."

The glow disappears before I can ask, "Where are the stairs?" Darn, these binarians are confusing. I stamp my foot in anger, but what the heck—I feel myself rise.

One step up, this is fun. Two, three … oops, I mean 10, 11 …

$1 = 1_2$	9 =	17 =	25 =
$2 = 10_2$	10 =	18 =	26 =
$3 = 11_2$	11 =	19 =	27 =
4 =	12 =	20 =	28 =
5 =	13 =	21 =	29 =
6 =	14 =	22 =	30 =
7 =	15 =	23 =	31 =
8 =	16 =	24 =	32 =

Well, look at this. I see a pattern.

$$100_2 = \underline{\hspace{2cm}}_{10}$$

$$1000_2 = \underline{\hspace{2cm}}_{10}$$

$$10000_2 = \underline{\hspace{2cm}}_{10}$$

$$100000_2 = \underline{\hspace{2cm}}_{10}$$

So after 100000 steps, I'm floating up really high. The orange glow returns.

"Proceed eastward 11011 footsteps."

I assume east is toward their star-rise. Walking on air is a little unsettling, but what choice do I have? How many steps do I need to take?

$$11011_2 = \underline{\hspace{2cm}}_{10}$$

Okay, I'm here. Still floating. A green mist appears in front of me and gradually solidifies into a door. They'll never believe this back home when I tell them. I cautiously open the door and find myself in a room very much like the ones on Earth back in the 21st century.

After floating through the air and finally passing through a door, who do you think is standing there waiting for me? Zero-One.

"You've functioned in our number system ... This is true."

"No trouble," I fib.

"Before we give you plutonium fuel, we need to ask you questions."

"What kind of questions? I don't reveal government secrets." (Plus I don't know any.) Darn! I forgot they can read my mind.

"Do not worry. We do not torture. We only ask that you fill out this survey about your species."

"No problem." I start to write my answers.

INTERPLANETARY SURVEY

NUMBER OF

PLANET OF ORIGIN EARTH

HEADS	1	GILLS	0	SLIME PORES	0
ANTENNAE	0	HEARTS	1	TEETH	32
ARMS	2	LUNGS	2	NOSTRILS	2
TENTACLES	0	SNOUTS	1	TONGUES	1
LEGS	2	OONGORP	0	ZEVNERS	0
FINGERS	10	EYES	2	FLIPPERS	0
TOES	10	GROMP	0	FEET/HOOVES	2
MOUTHS	1	TAILS	0	SCHNADLE	0
WINGS	0	BIPTAPS	0	BEAKS	0

SUBTOTAL= 26   SUBTOTAL= 6   SUBTOTAL= 37

TOTAL 69

"Please convert."

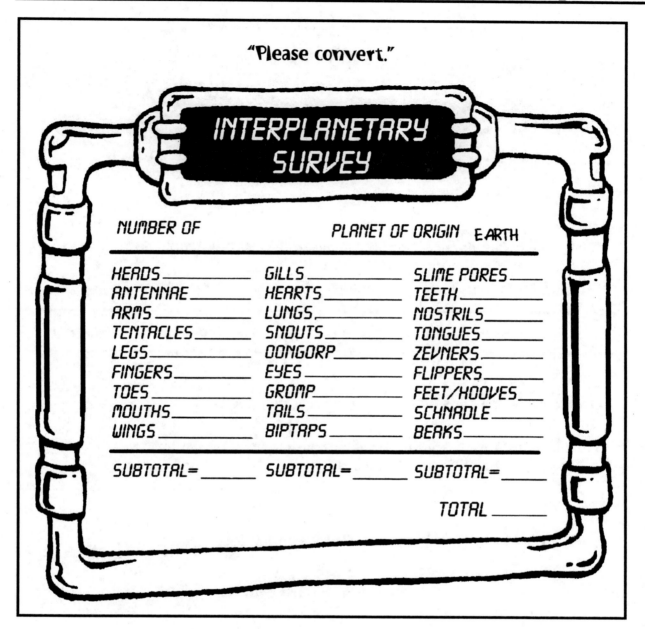

INTERPLANETARY SURVEY

NUMBER OF   PLANET OF ORIGIN   EARTH

HEADS_____	GILLS_____	SLIME PORES____
ANTENNAE_____	HEARTS_____	TEETH_____
ARMS_____	LUNGS_____	NOSTRILS_____
TENTACLES_____	SNOUTS_____	TONGUES_____
LEGS_____	OONGORP_____	ZEVNERS_____
FINGERS_____	EYES_____	FLIPPERS_____
TOES_____	GROMP_____	FEET/HOOVES___
MOUTHS_____	TAILS_____	SCHNADLE_____
WINGS_____	BIPTAPS_____	BEAKS_____

SUBTOTAL=_____   SUBTOTAL=_____   SUBTOTAL=_____

TOTAL_____

I complete my interplanetary survey and hand it over to Zero-One.

"Very good. Now, do you know the capacity of your fuel tank?"

"Without a hole in it? 60 pellets. Oops."

60_{10} **pellets = _____$_2$ pellets**

"Each cylinder contains 101 pellets. Take what you need."

I'm not sure how I'm going to get these back to the star-scooter. I can carry 4 cylinders easily. How many pellets can I carry?

$\qquad$ 101_2 **in the 1st cylinder**

$\qquad$ $+\,101_2$ **in the 2nd cylinder**

= $\qquad$ _____$_2$

$\qquad$ $+\,101_2$ **in the 3rd cylinder**

= $\qquad$ _____$_2$

$\qquad$ $+\,101_2$ **in the 4th cylinder**

= $\qquad$ _____$_2$ **total pellets**

I suppose I could have multiplied 4 x 101_2. Of course, the Binarians wouldn't use 4—they would use 100_2.

100_2 # of cylinders

x 101_2 pellets/ cylinders

_____

= _____$_2$ total pellets

Obviously, I need more pellets. How many more pellets do I need?

60_{10} pellets = _____$_2$ pellets

minus _____$_2$ pellets

equals _____$_2$ pellets

It wasn't that hard to multiply Binarian, so it shouldn't be that hard to divide. If I need 111100_2 pellets, and each cylinder contains 101_2 pellets, then the total number of cylinders I need is:

$$101_2 \overline{)111100_2}$$

If I can carry 100_2 cylinders in one trip,
how many trips back to the star-scooter will I have to make?

$$\underline{\hspace{2cm}}_2 \enclose{longdiv}{\underline{\hspace{3cm}}}_2 = \underline{\hspace{2.5cm}}_{10} \textbf{ trips}$$

I now have all the fuel I need, but how am I going to get all this stuff back to the star-scooter without making a lot of trips?

"Don't worry. We'll exlocate the fuel when we exlocate you. Are you ready?"

"Wait! Is there a place where I can buy some souvenirs before I go?"

"Try the galactic mall."

"Sure. Where is it?"

Poof!

This exlocation business is really slick. What a mall! Look at that. One head is getting his hair cut while the other head eats. And over here … "Excuse me, what is that device your other head is wearing?"

"My other half doesn't like shopping, so Widjit is watching a video—*The Attack of the Trinarians.*"

"Cool! Where can I get one of those video visors to take back home?"

"I got mine at Orgplork's, but you may have this one. Squidjit says it decomposes my mind. This is true."

Widjit takes off the video visor and folds it into a tiny cube.

"Thanks a lot! You two are great." Widjit-Squidjit walks away looking a little baffled.

I go check out Orgplork's. There are some amazing models of their native creatures. There is the 10-footed Zaldupe model with an eye on each foot, for example. I buy one. It comes in a box.

Here are some cool T-shirts floating in formation. I've got to have this one. It has no armholes and two headholes and it says, "I went to an uncharted alien planet and all I got was this lousy T-shirt." And it really says it. Out loud.

"I'll take eight, I mean 1000_2." I wonder if all this stuff will fit in the cargo bay of my star-scooter. "Do you have a measuring device I can use for a minute?" He hands me a digital scanner that measures anything I point it at.

Measurement of the video visor: 111_2 cm per side

What is the volume of the video visor?
(Let's see if it's possible to multiply without converting back to base 10)

$$111_2$$
$$\underline{\text{x} \quad 111_2}$$
$$111_2$$
$$1110_2$$
$$\underline{11100_2}$$
$$110001_2 = (111_2)^2 \text{ cm}^2$$
$$\underline{\text{x} \quad 111_2}$$

$$\underline{\hspace{2cm}}$$

$$\underline{\hspace{3cm}}_2 = (111_2)^3 \text{ cm}^3$$

Measurement of the Zaldupe box: 100 cm per side.

What is the volume of the Zaldupe box using base 2?
This is so simple, no need to multiply long hand.
$$(100_2)^3 = \underline{\hspace{2cm}}_2 \text{ cm}^3$$

Measurement of the T-shirt box: 1110 cm per side.

What is the volume of the T-shirt box using base 2?

$$1110_2$$

$$\underline{\times \quad 1110_2}$$

$$\underline{\qquad\qquad}_2$$
$$\underline{\qquad\qquad}_2 = (1110_2)^2 \text{ cm}^2$$
$$\underline{\times \quad 1110_2}$$

$$\underline{\qquad\qquad}_2$$
$$\underline{\qquad\qquad}_2 = (1110_2)^3 \text{ cm}^3$$

I have 3200 cubic centimeters of space left in the vehicle.
Can I take all three boxes?
If so, how much room is left for any other packages?

$$(111_2)^3 \quad = \underline{\qquad\qquad}_2 \text{ cm}^3 \text{ (video visor box)}$$

$$(100_2)^3 \quad = \underline{\qquad\qquad}_2 \text{ cm}^3 \text{ (Zaldupe box)}$$

$$+ \quad (1110_2)^3 \quad = \underline{\qquad\qquad}_2 \text{ cm}^3 \text{ (T-shirt box)}$$

$$= \underline{\qquad\qquad}_2 \text{ cm}^3 \text{ (total volume of boxes)}$$

Now subtract.

$$3200_{10} \quad = \underline{\qquad\qquad}_2 \text{ cm}^3 \text{ (cargo space)}$$

$$- \underline{\qquad}_{10} \quad = \underline{\qquad\qquad}_2 \text{ cm}^3 \text{ (boxes)}$$

$$\underline{\qquad}_{10} \quad = \underline{\qquad\qquad}_2 \text{ cm}^3 \text{ (cargo space remaining)}$$

STARLOG 2200

I'm back! I've got the star-scooter, the fuel pellets, and, most importantly, the souvenirs. Looks like saving the planet will be no problem. Mr. Alien! It's so good to see a familiar (sort of) face.

"The repairs to your fuel tank are completed. However, your vector guidance system is dysfunctional. Repair will require a visit to the Hexadecimites. They have a museum of ancient computers and should be able to assist you."

"What is a Hexa-"

I was going to ask Mr. Alien what kind of number system the Hexadecimites use, but it's too late now. Anyway, it's got to be simpler than base 2 or base 6 both of which I handled with ease.

Oh, boy. Here they come. Sixteen suction cups protruding from an octagonal orb rolling toward me. I can hardly wait.

"Welcome to our museum. I understand you are looking for some ancient computer parts. How may I help you?"

How do they use a keyboard, being orbs and all? I ask politely, "How do you coordinate 16 different suction cups on a keyboard?"

The hexadecimite laughs.

"Sorry, I thought you were joking. Keyboards have been obsolete for centuries. And what do you mean by 16 appendages? We have 10 appendages."

"Now wait a minute. I clearly count 16 appendages."

"Oh? Let's count. 1, 2, 3, 4, 5, 6, 7, 8, 9, A, B, C, D, E, F, 10."

No fair. You can't use letters for numbers.

"Oh?"

And you can't have more than 10.

"We don't."

You know, the Earth may end up being a hyperspace traffic lane after all.

"I understand you need some fiber-optic transponders for your directional modules. Proceed to the 12th chamber on your left and you'll find what you need."

I'm counting chambers. 1, 2, 3, …, 11, 12. This must be it. What the heck is this?

You've never seen anything until you've seen a hexadecimite's restroom.

> **Anyway, this is not the 12th chamber.**
> **Where did I go wrong?**
> 12_{16}= _____$_{10}$?

After figuring out that the hexadecimites use base 16, I am able to find the 12th chamber. It is not a restroom. I find a museum assistant painting its 16 suction cups in random colors.

Now let me think, I have 6 directional modules, and each one needs 5 fiber-optic transponders.

How many transponders do I ask for?

$30_{10} = $ _____ $_{16}$

"Normally, we only send fiber-optic transponders for educational purposes—ancient history classes, for example. Therefore we must ask that you pay a nominal fee of D spornks for each transponder."

"You've got to be kidding! You expect me to multiply D by 1E ?" Earth is in *serious* danger!

I guess the only way to get started is to make a multiplication table for base 16.

x	1	2	3	4	5	6	7	8	9	A	B	C	D	E	F	10
1	1	2	3	4	5	6	7	8	9	A	B	C	D	E	F	10
2	2	4	6	8	A	C	E	10	12	14	16	18	1A	1C	1E	20
3	3	6	9													
4	4	8														
5	5	A														
6	6	C														
7	7	E														
8	8	10														
9	9	12														
A	A	14														
B	B	16														
C	C	18														
D	D	1A														
E	E	1C														
F	F	1E														
10	10	20														

Hours later, "Isn't there an easier way to multiply D by 1E ?"

"There is a simple way to multiply in our system, developed through scientific collaboration with the Binarians. Remember how easy it is to multiply in binary? Each hexadecimal number has an equivalent 4-digit binary number. Convert to binary, then multiply."

Sounds too simple. "How do you convert a hexademical number to its 4-digit binary equivalent?"

"Count in binary."

"0, 1, 10, 11—"

"Remember, each one has to be 4 digits long."

"Okay ... 0000, 0001, 0010, 0011, 0100, 0101, 0110, 0111, 1000, 1001, 1010, 1011, 1100, 1101, 1110, 1111. That's as far as I can go in four digits."

"What are those numbers in hexadecimal?"

Let's see:

0000_2 is _____ 0_{16}	1000_2 is _____ $_{16}$
0001_2 is _____ 1_{16}	1001_2 is _____ $_{16}$
0010_2 is _____ $_{16}$	1010_2 is _____ $_{16}$
0011_2 is _____ $_{16}$	1011_2 is _____ $_{16}$
0100_2 is _____ $_{16}$	1100_2 is _____ $_{16}$
0101_2 is _____ $_{16}$	1101_2 is _____ $_{16}$
0110_2 is _____ $_{16}$	1110_2 is _____ $_{16}$
0111_2 is _____ $_{16}$	1111_2 is _____ $_{16}$

"So you see, 1€ can be written as 0001 1110₂. Now multiply to find out how many spornks you need to pay for the transponders."

$$00001\ 1110_2\ =\ \underline{\quad\textbf{1E}\quad}_{16}$$

$$\underline{x\qquad 1101}_2\ =\ \underline{x\qquad \textbf{D}\qquad}_{16}$$

$$\underline{\qquad\qquad\qquad}_2\ =\ \underline{\qquad\qquad}_{16}\ \textbf{spornks (transponders)}$$

"Is there anything else?"

"Now that you mention it, I could use an antimatter detector."

"I'm so sorry, the museum only has a few—"

"That's okay, no matter."

"But in your case, we'll make an exception. They're kind of expensive. That will be BAD spornks."

"How bad?"

"Not 'bad' the word, BAD the number!"

It's been much too long a day.

> ## "How many spornks do I owe?"
> **BAD$_{16}$ spornks (antimatter detector)**
>
> + _____$_{16}$ **spornks (transponders)**
>
> _____$_{16}$ **total spornks**

"Do you accept roogegs?"

"Naturally. One roogeg is the same as f spornks."

"Gimme a break. Now I need to divide the total spornks I owe by F$_{16}$? Good grief. I suppose I should write each hexadecimal number as a 4-digit binary number?"

"Precisely! You are learning quickly."

"Fine, I'll give it a try."

$$1111_2 \overline{)1101\ 0011\ 0011_2}$$

Three hours later and 17 pages later in my spacelog, I have some kind of answer. Meanwhile, the museum assistant, who has been analyzing the vocalization of Uravian glordelia flies asks me,

"Did you get a remainder of 100?"

"Yes!" I leap up, forgetting that the gravity on this planet is less than that on Earth, and whack my head on the ceiling.

"Now, work the problem out to two places beyond the hexadecimal point."

"Hexadecimal point?" I ask weakly. As much as I want to save the Earth …

"Cheer up, old chap, it is in every respect the same as your decimal point. You can do it. Work out to three places, then decide whether to round up or down."

"And if I figure it out?"

"You will have my respect."

"Respect? Okay, you're on … but I'm out of paper and I can't remember what the problem was."

"You were dividing the D33 spornks you owe by f in order to convert to roogegs. Try this three-dimensional glow pen.

Awesome pen—it writes in the air. "When I'm done, I'll know how many roogegs I owe, right?"

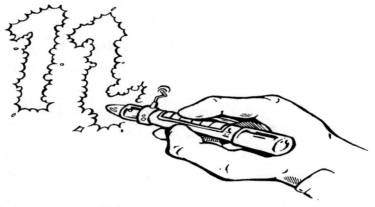

$$1111_2 \overline{)1101\ 0011\ 0011.0000\ 0000\ 0000_2}$$

**To round up or round down, that is the question.
If the third hexadecimal place is _____$_{16}$, I should round up.**

"Extraordinary. Such intelligence is rare amongst inhabitants of the Milky Way, I'm sure. You are a credit to your galaxy."

I hand the museum assistant a 300_{10}-roogeg note.

How much change should I receive to two hexadecimal places?

$\underline{\hspace{3cm}}.00_{16} = 300_{10}$ roogegs

$-\underline{\hspace{2.5cm}}.\underline{\hspace{0.8cm}}_{16} =$ roogegs I owe two hexadecimal places

$\underline{\hspace{2.5cm}}.\underline{\hspace{0.8cm}}_{16} =$ change in roogegs to two hexadecimal places

---

The assistant's Bth suction cup inhales the money and spits out the change. "Did I do it? Did I save the Earth? Can I go home now?"

"I can neither confirm nor deny the possibility."

"Then can you help me get back to my star-scooter? I have no idea where I am."

"Certainly. And may I say, it has been a pleasure to meet someone so—how should I say—elemental."

STARLOG 2500

"Mr. Alien! Am I finished yet?"

"You have proven to be an interesting specimen; one worthy of study. We are impressed with the fact that you have not given up despite the difficulties one encounters negotiating alternate number systems."

"Thanks. It's been real."

"Yes, you have succeeded in counting, converting, adding, and subtracting in all the bases so far. Furthermore, we have observed your ability to multiply and divide in binary and hexadecimal."

Suddenly I realize I never tried multiplication or division in base 6. I look into his eyes and know what's next. "I want to try it."

He looks at me with something akin to respect. I hope.

"Let's talk about time. Here, there are 5 melborp in each snalpf, 3 snalpf in each yeoof (based on the orbit of our largest moon) and of course 45 yeoof in each year."

"So let me guess, you want me to calculate the number of melborp in a year. Well, at least the first part is easy."

$$5_6 \text{ melborp } \times 3_6 \text{ snalpf} = \underline{\hspace{2cm}}_6 \text{ melborp}$$

But then I have a double digit number times a double digit! Sweat begins to trickle down my forehead.

"It is suggested, due to the suspected limits of Milky Wayan mental capacity, that you make a multiplication table. First, you must ..."

"Don't help me ... I can do this."

X	1	2	3	4	5	10	11	12
1								
2								
3								
4								
5								
10								
11								
12								

"What was the problem? Oh yeah, ..."

$$5_6 \text{ melborp/snalpf}$$
$$\text{x} \quad 3_6 \text{ \underline{snalpf/yeoof}}$$
$$\underline{\quad\quad}_6 \text{ melborp/yeoof}$$
$$\text{x} \quad 45_6 \text{ yeoof/year}$$

$$\underline{\quad\quad\quad\quad}$$

$$\underline{\quad\quad}_6 \text{ melborp/year}$$

"Is that it? Will you admit it? Have I proven Earthlings are intelligent?"

"There is one more complication. We brought your space-scooter in through a Milky Way time warp. That means you can only return in a time warp. You understand."

I'm enraged! "You got me here! You'd better have some way of getting me back! When is the next time warp, anyway?"

"Well, a corridor in the time warp occurs approximately every 5 melborp. In one year, how many time warps would be expected?"

"I can do that."

$$\underline{}_6)\overline{_6} \quad \frac{}{}_6 = \underline{}_{10} \textbf{ time warps/year}$$

"Okay, about one every four days. Now, let me go home."

"Not so fast. Your analysis would be true if we were on your planet. But here, one year is equal to several of your millennia."

"Look! My superiors will be really alarmed if I don't return soon! And so will my parents!"

"Are you finished with this distasteful display of emotion?"

Well, how does he expect me to react? Stuck on this planet with a bunch of weirdos who don't even know how to count right, and they want to know if humans are intelligent! "Okay, I'm sorry. Please tell me how to get off this planet."

"I shall proceed. Our two galaxies' time warps align on rare occasion. Fortunately, such an alignment will occur in approximately 4.875 Earth minutes. You may prepare to disembark."

"That's it? I can go?"

"Unless you have an inclination to stay. I hope you do. I look forward to introducing you to the base one-half society."

"No! I mean, thanks for the offer, but I really need to go home now."

I walk out of the building heading for my space-scooter, which is all loaded, fueled, and even washed.

Zero-One (or was it One-Zero?) and a number of the other aliens I encountered are waving to me. There are even a few I don't know, and through the cheering, I hear a few trying to convince me to stay a bit longer.

I make sure to close the hatch before the one with twelve 12-fingered hands comes near. Bye, guys.

The answers to all problems are given with explanations immediately following those problems whose answers may not be readily understood.

STARLOG 1900

How do I count in base 6?

$1 = 1_6$	$7 = 11_6$	$13 = 21_6$	$19 = 31_6$	$25 = 41_6$	$31 = 51_6$
$2 = 2_6$	$8 = 12_6$	$14 = 22_6$	$20 = 32_6$	$26 = 42_6$	$32 = 52_6$
$3 = 3_6$	$9 = 13_6$	$15 = 23_6$	$21 = 33_6$	$27 = 43_6$	$33 = 53_6$
$4 = 4_6$	$10 = 14_6$	$16 = 24_6$	$22 = 34_6$	$28 = 44_6$	$34 = 54_6$
$5 = 5_6$	$11 = 15_6$	$17 = 25_6$	$23 = 35_6$	$29 = 45_6$	$35 = 55_6$
$6 = 10_6$	$12 = 20_6$	$18 = 30_6$	$24 = 40_6$	$30 = 50_6$	$36 = 100_6$

How do we count in base 6? Would it help to examine counting in base 10? Let's see. Base 10 uses ten symbols, namely, 0, 1, 2, 3, 4, 5, 6, 7, 8, 9.

In base 10, what comes after 9, the last symbol? The next 10 numbers are two-digit beginning with 1 and the last digit goes through 0, …, 9, resulting in the numbers 10, …, 19. The leading digit changes to 2 and the last digit goes through 0, …, 9 resulting in the numbers 20, …, 29. Continue in this manner until 99 is reached and no more symbols are available. The next numbers are three-digit beginning with 1 and the last two digits go from 00, 01, to 99 resulting in the numbers 100, 101, …, 199. On and on it goes.

Let's count this way in base 6. Base 6 uses six symbols, namely, 0, 1, 2, 3, 4, 5.

In base 6, what numbers come after 5, the last symbol? The next six numbers are two-digit beginning with 1 and the last digit goes through 0, …, 5, resulting in the numbers 10, …, 15. The leading digit changes to 2 and the last digit goes through 0, …, 5, resulting in the numbers 20, …, 25. Continue in this manner until 55 is reached and no more symbols are available. The next numbers are three-digit beginning with 1 and the last two digits go from 00, 01, to 55 resulting in the numbers 100, 101, …., 155. On and on it goes.

This method of counting applies to every number base.

If Mr. Alien says 10, what does that mean to me? $10_6 = \underline{6^1 = 6}_{10}$

If he says 100? $100_6 = \underline{6^2 = 36}_{10}$

If he says 1000? $1000_6 = \underline{6^3 = 216}_{10}$

If he says 10000? $10000_6 = \underline{6^4 = 1296}_{10}$

Hint:

For each power of the base, the exponent equals the number of zeroes following a digit of one. For example, $6^2 = 100_6$ has an exponent of two and two zeroes follow a digit of one.

In base 10, there is the ones place, the tens place, the hundreds place and so on. Why?

The reason is that $10^0 = 1$, $10^1 = 10$, $10^2 = 100$, $10^3 = 1000$. That's why. In any base, all place-values are powers of the base. Understand this, and you will understand the rest of the book.

$$72_{10} = \underline{200}_6$$

The place of the digit determines its value. For base 6, the place-values are:

$$6^3 = 216 \qquad 6^2 = 36 \qquad 6^1 = 6 \qquad 6^0 = 1$$

Ask yourself, for the number 72_{10}, what is the largest power of 6 that does not exceed 72_{10}? The answer is 36, so the number will be three-digits. But how many 36s are in 72? There are 2 exactly, so the answer must be 200_6.

$$55_{10} = \underline{131}_6$$

Converting 72 is pretty easy, but converting 55 is a little more difficult.

How many 36s are in 55? There is **1** with a remainder of 19.
How many 6s are in 19? There are **3** with a remainder of 1.
How many units are in 1? There is **1**.

$$113_{10} = \underline{305}_6?$$

$113 \div 36 = \mathbf{3}$ with a remainder of 5
$5 \div 6 = \mathbf{0}$ with a remainder of 5
$5 \div 1 = \mathbf{5}$

This method is a drag because powers of 6 must be found beforehand. That's not too bad for 113, but what about 34,587?

This method is the most understandable way to convert a number to another base, but it is definitely not the most practical.

What is wrong with this method? **It works backward!** It finds the leading digit first and moves to the right until it gets to the units digit.

When adding, subtracting, or multiplying, do we start with the leading digits? No! We start with the units digit. **When converting from base 10 to another number base, it is much more efficient to start with the units digit.**

How do we find the units digit first? How do we find the other digits?

We use a method we call the repeated-division method. "Above and Beyond" in the *Space Traveler's Training Manual* asks the students to derive a better method of conversion, so you may decide not to share the repeated-division method with the students until they have had a chance to discover it themselves.

How Does the Repeated-Division Method Work?

The following is an attempt to explain how the repeated-division method works. Hopefully, it is understandable. Don't get stressed if it doesn't makes sense. Knowing how the repeated-division method works is not essential to using it.

Let's consider the number 113_{10}. What is the units digit in base 6? It should be what is left over when 113 is divided by 6.

$113 \div 6 = 18$ with a remainder of **5**

So far, $113_{10} =$ ____5_6 leaving a blank for the unknown digits.

The quotient of *18* means there are 18 sets of 6s in 113, so is *18* the digit for the place-value of 6 resulting in $113_{10} = 185_6$? **No!** Why not? First, **the symbol *8* does not exist in base 6**, and second, *18* **is not a single digit.**

What now? Find the equivalent of 18 in base 6. Of course, it is easy to determine that $18_{10} = \mathbf{30_6}$. To convert larger numbers, however, the last digit would be the remainder when dividing by 6. Continuing with this example,

$18 \div 6 = 3$ with a remainder of **0**.

The quotient of 3 can be the digit for the place-value of 36 since it is a single digit existing in base 6. So far, the remainder, not the quotient, has been the desired digit. Is this an inconsistency? No. If the last quotient of *3* is divided by 6, the quotient of *3* will become a remainder of **3**.

$3 \div 6 = 0$ with a remainder of **3**

The quotient is *0*. To divide *0* by 6 would be a lesson in futility. Why? All subsequent divisions have a remainder of 0. A quotient of 0 means it is time to stop.

The remainders from dividing repeatedly by 6 are the digits in base 6 from right to left. Stop dividing when the quotient is 0.

Look again at converting 113_{10} to base 6 using the **repeated-division method**.

$113 \div 6 = 18$ with a remainder of **5**

$18 \div 6 = 3$ with a remainder of **0**

$3 \div 6 = 0$ with a remainder of **3**

Conclude $113_{10} =$ **305_6**.

Repeated-division converts to base 6 quicker because the powers of 6 are not needed.

Repeated-Division Method

Step 1: Divide the base 10 number by the desired base finding the remainder.
Step 2: Divide the quotient by the base finding the remainder.
Step 3: Continue in this manner until a quotient of 0 is reached.
Step 4: The remainders in reverse order are the digits of the number in the desired base.

We will use a shortened notation throughout the answer key. The intermediate steps are shown for this example but will not be shown in the remainder of the answer key.

Step 1: The first division is shown.

$$6\overline{)113} \quad 18 \text{ R } 5$$

Step 2: The second division is in italic.

$$6\overline{)18} \text{ R } 5 \quad 3 R 0$$
$$6\overline{)113}$$

Step 3: The final division is in italic.

$$6\overline{)3} R 0 \quad 0 R 3$$
$$6\overline{)18} \text{ R } 5$$
$$6\overline{)113}$$

This shortened notation is nice since the digits are in order from top to bottom.

Need to convert a base 10 number to base 5? Divide repeatedly by 5 instead of 6.

The first problem of Starlog 1500 in the "Space Traveler's Training Manual" requires the students to use the repeated-division method to convert base 10 numbers to various other bases.

STARLOG 1500

$$1435_6 = \underline{383}_{10}$$

Keep in mind that each place-value is a power of 6.

Do you remember our hint? **The power of 6 always equals the number of digits following that number.** Three digits follow the **1**, so the place-value is $6^3 = 216$. There is **one** *216*.

Two digits follow the 4, so the place-value is $6^2 = 36$. There are **four** 36s, which is **4** x 36 = *144*.

One digit follows the **3**, so the place-value is $6^1 = 6$. There are **three** 6s, which is **3** x 6 = *18*.

No digits follow the **5**, so the place-value is $6^0 = 1$. There are **five** ones, which is **5** x 1=*5*.

Add all the numbers in italic.

$$216 + 144 + 18 + 5 = \mathbf{383}.$$

Is there a shorter process? Try this.

$$
\begin{array}{l}
\mathbf{1} \times 6^3 = \mathbf{1} \times 216 = \mathit{216} \\
\mathbf{4} \times 6^2 = \mathbf{4} \times 36 = \mathit{144} \\
\mathbf{3} \times 6^1 = \mathbf{3} \times 6 = \mathit{18} \\
\mathbf{5} \times 6^0 = \mathbf{5} \times 1 = \underline{\mathit{5}} \\
\hline
\mathbf{383}
\end{array}
$$

$$432_6 = \underline{\textbf{164}}_{10}$$

$$
\begin{aligned}
\textbf{4} \times 6^2 &= \textbf{4} \times 36 = \mathit{144}\\
\textbf{3} \times 6^1 &= \textbf{3} \times6 = \mathit{18}\\
\underline{\textbf{2} \times 6^0 = \textbf{2} \times1 = \mathit{2}}\\
\textbf{164}
\end{aligned}
$$

This is a good time to introduce the students to some algebraic notation. Algebraic notation writes the previous more concisely as

$$432_6 = 4(6^2) + 3(6^1) + 2(6^0) = 4(36) + 3(6) + 2(1) = 144 + 18 + 2 = \textbf{164}_{10}.$$

Omitting "x" allows 4×6^2 to be written as $4(6^2)$, $(4)(6^2)$, or $(4)6^2$. At least one set of parentheses is essential. Why? Without parentheses, 46^2 would be interpreted as 46 to the second power. For expressions such as 4×6^2, the customary notation, $4(6)^2$, has been written as $4(6^2)$ to emphasize the base is squared before multiplying by 4.

How much does each dish cost in base 10?	
Horndabber with Rotsa	33_6 roogegs = $\underline{\textbf{21}}_{10}$
Glooglib	14_6 roogegs = $\underline{\textbf{10}}_{10}$
Hinkledamper	42_6 roogegs = $\underline{\textbf{26}}_{10}$
Corgle	125_6 roogegs = $\underline{\textbf{53}}_{10}$
Zoople	152_6 roogegs = $\underline{\textbf{68}}_{10}$
Koojee	51_6 roogegs = $\underline{\textbf{31}}_{10}$
Porveq	44_6 roogegs = $\underline{\textbf{28}}_{10}$
Handerschnap	131_6 roogegs = $\underline{\textbf{55}}_{10}$
with Moorgley	202_6 roogegs = $\underline{\textbf{74}}_{10}$

Answer Key

$$33_6 = 3(6^1) + 3(6^0) = 3(6) + 3(1) = 18 + 3 = 21_{10}$$
$$14_6 = 1(6^1) + 4(6^0) = 1(6) + 4(1) = 6 + 4 = 10_{10}$$
$$42_6 = 4(6^1) + 2(6^0) = 4(6) + 2(1) = 24 + 2 = 26_{10}$$
$$125_6 = 1(6^2) + 2(6^1) + 5(6^0) = 1(36) + 2(6) + 5(1) = 36 + 12 + 5 = 53_{10}$$
$$152_6 = 1(6^2) + 5(6^1) + 2(6^0) = 1(36) + 5(6) + 2(1) = 36 + 30 + 2 = 68_{10}$$
$$51_6 = 5(6^1) + 1(6^0) = 5(6) + 1(1) = 30 + 1 = 31_{10}$$
$$44_6 = 4(6^1) + 4(6^0) = 4(6) + 4(1) = 24 + 4 = 28_{10}$$
$$131_6 = 1(6^2) + 3(6^1) + 1(6^0) = 1(36) + 3(6) + 1(1) = 36 + 18 + 1 = 55_{10}$$
$$202_6 = 2(6^2) + 0(6^1) + 2(6^0) = 2(36) + 0(6) + 2(1) = 72 + 0 + 2 = 74_{10}$$

How much do I owe for the glooglib, horndabber with rotsa, and the handerschnap? (He didn't charge me for the moorgley.)

10_{10}	roogegs for the glooglib
21_{10}	roogegs for the horndabber with rotsa
55_{10}	roogegs for the handerschnap
86_{10}	**Total cost in roogegs**

100_{10}	**roogegs**
86_{10}	**total cost in roogegs**
14_{10}	**change in roogegs**

I left a tip of 22_6 roogegs. I hope it's enough.

> 3_6 **roogegs for the 1st box of sock cookies**
> $+ \ 3_6$ **roogegs for the 2nd box of sock cookies**
>
> 10_6 **Total cost for 2 boxes of sock cookies**

Tell students not to use base 10 as an intermediate step.

Students are using base 10 as an intermediate step when they say 3 + 3 is 6 which is 10_6.

So how do we add in base 6 without using base 10 as an intermediate step?

To add in base 10, we learned the addition facts for base 10. Similarly, adding in base 6 requires learning the addition facts for base 6. Okay, how can the addition facts for base 6 be derived?

Examining how addition facts for base 10 are found might give us an idea how to find the addition facts for base 6.

In base 10, what does 4 + 9 really mean? It says to start with 4 and count up 9 units. First-graders figure out 4 + 9 = 13 by counting on their fingers as follows:

4 5 6 7 8 9 10 11 12 **13**
[counting up 9 units to 13]

Finding the addition facts for base 6 is done the same way **except the counting is done in base 6.**

What is $3_6 + 3_6$? Start at 3_6 and count up 3_6 units in base 6.

3_6 4_6 5_6 10_6 So, $3_6 + 3_6 = 10_6$.
[up 3_6 units]

What is $4_6 + 5_6$? Start at 4_6 and count up 5_6 units in base 6.

4_6 5_6 10_6 11_6 12_6 $\textbf{13}_6$ So, $4_6 + 5_6 = 13_6$.
[count up 5_6 units]

The addition facts for base 6 are summarized in the following table.

Base 6 Addition Table

+	1	2	3	4	5
1	2	3	4	5	10
2	3	4	5	10	11
3	4	5	10	11	12
4	5	10	11	12	13
5	10	11	12	13	14

Note: Although the sums in the table are symmetric about the main diagonal, all are given to demonstrate that the commutative property of addition (2 + 3 = 3 + 2) still holds for addition in other bases.

Students will soon add without an addition table by "making 10_6." Adding $4_6 + 5_6$ can be thought of as $(4_6 + 2_6) + 3_6 = 13_6$, just as 7 + 6 can be thought of as (7 + 3) + 3 = 13.

$$
\begin{array}{rl}
10_6 & \text{roogegs for the 2 boxes of sock cookies} \\
+\ 25_6 & \text{roogegs for the pig feet} \\
\hline
35_6 & \text{Total cost so far}
\end{array}
$$

$$
\begin{array}{rl}
35_6 & \text{roogegs for sock cookies and pig feet} \\
+\ 50_6 & \text{roogegs for 5 gallons of chocolate ice cream} \\
\hline
125_6 & \text{Total cost for everything}
\end{array}
$$

$$100_{10} \text{ roogegs} = 244_6 \text{ roogegs}$$
$$\text{minus} \quad 125_6 \text{ total cost}$$
$$\text{equals} \quad 115_6 \text{ change in roogegs}$$

What is $14_6 - 5_6$? Start at 14_6 and count **down** 5_6 units in base six.

14_6 13_6 12_6 11_6 10_6 5_6 So, $14_6 - 5_6 = 5_6$.
[count down 5_6 units]

For subtraction, the addition table can be used in reverse. Find 14_6 in row 5_6 and the column heading, 5_6, is the difference.

STARLOG 1700

Starlogs 1700 through 2400 are the most important. Why? These Starlogs pertain to base 2 and base 16, otherwise known as binary and hexadecimal, the computer bases.

Starlogs 1700 and 1800 may be discussed on the same day.

So if they only have two numbers, 0 and 1, then $2_{10} = \underline{10}_2$

By this time, students should understand counting in any base. If they do not, emphasize that base 2 has only two symbols, namely 0 and 1. The place-values are now powers of 2.

I had better learn to count in Binarian.

$0 = 0_2$	$1 = 1_2$	$2 = 10_2$	$3 = 11_2$	$4 = 100_2$
$5 = 101_2$	$6 = 110_2$	$7 = 111_2$	$8 = 1000_2$	$9 = 1001_2$

If a base 10 number is even, what is the last digit of the number in binary? Zero. If a base 10 number is odd, what is the last digit of the number in binary? One.

Do I get off here or not?
$$1010_2 = \underline{10}_{10}$$

The method using algebraic notation in the answer key for Starlog 1500 converts numbers in **any base** to base 10. Change the base to the current base of the number. The base is 2 in this problem, so

$$1010_2 = 1(2^3) + 0(2^2) + 1(2^1) + 0(2^0) = 1(8) + 0(4) + 1(2) + 0(1) = 8 + 2 = 10_{10}.$$

STARLOG 1800

$1 = 1_2$	$9 = 1001_2$	$17 = 10001_2$	$25 = 11001_2$
$2 = 10_2$	$10 = 1010_2$	$18 = 10010_2$	$26 = 11010_2$
$3 = 11_2$	$11 = 1011_2$	$19 = 10011_2$	$27 = 11011_2$
$4 = 100_2$	$12 = 1100_2$	$20 = 10100_2$	$28 = 11100_2$
$5 = 101_2$	$13 = 1101_2$	$21 = 10101_2$	$29 = 11101_2$
$6 = 110_2$	$14 = 1110_2$	$22 = 10110_2$	$30 = 11110_2$
$7 = 111_2$	$15 = 1111_2$	$23 = 10111_2$	$31 = 11111_2$
$8 = 1000_2$	$16 = 10000_2$	$24 = 11000_2$	$32 = 100000_2$

$$100_2 = \underline{2^2} = \underline{4}_{10}$$

$$1000_2 = \underline{2^3} = \underline{8}_{10}$$

$$10000_2 = \underline{2^4} = \underline{16}_{10}$$

$$100000_2 = \underline{2^5} = \underline{32}_{10}$$

$$11011_2 = \underline{27}_{10}$$

$$11011_2 = 1(2^4) + 1(2^3) + 0(2^2) + 1(2^1) + 1(2^0) = 1(16) + 1(8) + 0(4) + 1(2) + 1(1)$$
$$= 16 + 8 + 2 + 1 = 27_{10}$$

STARLOG 1900

Interplanetary Survey					
Number of				**Planet of origin: Earth**	
heads	1_2	gills	0_2	slime pores	0_2
antennae	0_2	hearts	1_2	teeth	100000_2
arms	10_2	lungs	10_2	nostrils	10_2
tentacles	0_2	snouts	1_2	tongues	1_2
legs	10_2	oongorp	0_2	zevners	0_2
fingers	1010_2	eyes	10_2	flippers	0_2
toes	1010_2	gromp	0_2	feet/hooves	10_2
mouths	1_2	tails	0_2	schnadle	0_2
wings	0_2	biptaps	0_2	beaks	0_2
subtotal =	11010_2	subtotal =	110_2	subtotal =	100101_2
				Total=	1000101_2

The binary equivalents of 1_{10}, 2_{10}, 6_{10}, 10_{10}, and 32_{10} have already been determined.

The conversions of 26_{10}, 37_{10}, and 69_{10} to binary using the repeated-division method are shown.

```
                                                              0 R 1
                                                          2 ) 1 R 0
                                      0 R 1               2 ) 2 R 0
                0 R 1             2 ) 1 R 0               2 ) 4 R 0
            2 ) 1 R 1             2 ) 2 R 0               2 ) 8 R 1
            2 ) 3 R 0             2 ) 4 R 1               2 ) 17 R 0
            2 ) 6 R 0             2 ) 9 R 0               2 ) 34 R 1
            2 ) 13 R 1            2 ) 18 R 1              2 ) 69
            2 ) 26                2 ) 37
```

So, $26_{10} = 11010_2$
        $37_{10} = 100101_2$
        $69_{10} = 1000101_2$.

60_{10} pellets = $\underline{111100_2}$ pellets

With 2 as the divisor, make the conversion using repeated-division.

101_2 **in the 1st cylinder**

$+$ 101_2 **in the 2nd cylinder**

$=$ 1010_2

$+$ 101_2 **in the 3rd cylinder**

$=$ 1111_2

$+$ 101_2 **in the 4th cylinder**

$=$ 10100_2 **total pellets**

The addition facts for binary couldn't be easier. "Carry" as usual.

$$0 + 0 = 0$$
$$0 + 1 = 1$$
$$1 + 1 = 10$$

100_2 **# of cylinders**

x 101_2 **pellets/cylinders**

100

0000

$\underline{10000}$

$= 10100_2$ **total pellets**

Multiplication in binary is even easier than addition.

$$0 \times 0 = 0$$
$$0 \times 1 = 0$$
$$1 \times 1 = 1$$

$$60_{10} \text{ pellets} = 111100_2 \text{ pellets}$$
$$\text{minus} \quad 10100_2 \text{ pellets}$$
$$\text{equals} \quad 101000_2 \text{ pellets}$$

Subtract as usual. There is no need to "borrow."

$$
\begin{array}{r}
1100_2 \\
101_2 \overline{)\ 111100_2} \\
\underline{101} \\
101 \\
\underline{101} \\
0
\end{array}
$$

Divide preceding and following problems as usual. The subtractions require no borrowing.

If I can carry 100_2 cylinders in one trip, how many trips back to the star-scooter will I have to make?

$$
\begin{array}{r}
11_2 = 3_{10} \text{ trips} \\
100_2 \overline{)\ 1100_2} \\
\underline{100} \\
100 \\
\underline{100} \\
0
\end{array}
$$

What is the volume of the video visor?
(Let's see if it's possible to multiply without converting back to base 10)

$$111_2$$
$$\underline{x \qquad 111_2}$$
$$111_2$$
$$1110_2$$
$$\underline{11100_2}$$
$$110001_2 = (111_2)^2 \text{ cm}^2$$
$$\underline{x \qquad 111_2}$$
$$110001$$
$$1100010$$
$$\underline{11000100}$$
$$101010111_2 = (111_2)^3 \text{ cm}^3$$

Multiply as usual. Remember to add in binary.

What is the volume of the Zaldupe box using base 2?
This is so simple, no need to multiply long-hand.
$$(100_2)^3 = 1000000_2 \text{ cm}^3$$

It is interesting that the third power has three times as many zeroes. How many zeroes would there be for the fourth power? Eight zeroes, four times as many.

What is the volume of the T-shirt box using base 2?

$$
\begin{array}{r}
1110_2 \\
\times \quad 1110_2 \\
\hline
0000 \\
11100 \\
111000 \\
1110000 \\
\hline
11000100_2 = (1110_2)^2 \text{cm}^2 \\
\times \quad 1110_2 \\
\hline
0000 \\
110001000 \\
1100010000 \\
11000100000 \\
\hline
101010111000_2 = (1110_2)^3 \text{cm}^3
\end{array}
$$

The column in bold gives a sum of 100_2, so 10_2 must be carried.

Carries of two or more digits can be done in a couple of ways.

The third column of the following example has a two-digit carry.

$$
\begin{array}{r}
11101 \\
10111 \\
+ \quad 11110 \\
\end{array}
$$

One option is to take the two-digit carry to the next column as follows:

$$
\begin{array}{r}
10 \; 10 \; 1 \; 1 \\
11101 \\
10111 \\
+ \quad 11110 \\
\hline
1010010
\end{array}
$$

Another option is to **split the two-digit carry over the next two columns** as shown in bold. The sum of the second column from the left adds to 10_2, resulting in the carry of 1 in italic.

$$
\begin{array}{r}
\mathit{1} \\
\mathbf{1}\ \mathbf{0}\ \mathbf{1}\ \mathbf{1} \\
1 1 1 0 1 \\
1 0 1 1 1 \\
+\qquad 1 1 1 1 0 \\
\hline
1 0 1 0 0 1 0
\end{array}
$$

What about **three-digit** carries? Split the carry over the **next three columns**. Split four-digit to carries over to the next four columns, and so on.

I have 3200 cubic centimeters of space left in the vehicle.
Can I take all three boxes?
If so, how much room is left for any other packages?

$$
\begin{aligned}
(111_2)^3 &= 101010111_2 \text{ cm}^3 \text{ (video visor box)} \\
(100_2)^3 &= 1000000_2 \text{ cm}^3 \text{ (Zaldupe box)} \\
+\ (1110_2)^3 &= \underline{101010111000_2 \text{ cm}^3 \text{ (T-shirt box)}} \\
&= 110001001111_2 \text{ cm}^3 \text{ (total volume of boxes)}
\end{aligned}
$$

$$
\begin{aligned}
3200_{10} &= 110010000000_2 \text{ cm}^3 \text{ (cargo space)} \\
-\ 3151_{10} &= \underline{110001001111_2 \text{ cm}^3 \text{ (boxes)}} \\
49_{10} &= 000000110001_2 \text{ cm}^3 \text{ (cargo space remaining)}
\end{aligned}
$$

Borrowing from 1_2 is simple enough, but **borrowing from 0_2 is not possible**. However, **10_2 can be borrowed**.

For problems like (10000 – 3257), a 10 is borrowed from 10000 leaving 9990 as shown below.

$$
\begin{array}{r}
{\scriptstyle 0\ 9\ 9\ 9\ 10} \\
\cancel{10000} \\
-\quad 3257 \\
\hline
6743
\end{array}
$$

Once a 10 is borrowed, borrowing is continued until a nonzero number from which to borrow is reached.

Borrowing in binary is the same. Once a 10_2 is borrowed, keep borrowing until a 1_2 from which to borrow is reached.

All the borrows for the last problem of this Starlog are shown below.

$$
\begin{array}{r}
{\scriptstyle 0\ 1\ 1\ 1\ 1\ 1\ 1\ 10} \\
1100\cancel{10000000} \\
-\quad 110001001111 \\
\hline
000000110001
\end{array}
$$

"Adding back" checks subtraction in any base. All binary subtractions should be checked since "adding back" is so easy.

STARLOG 2200

Anyway, this is not the 12th chamber. Where did I go wrong?
$$12_{16} = \underline{18}_{10}?$$

Referring to Starlog 1500 answer key, use the algebraic notation with the base as 16 to convert to base 10.

$$12_{16} = 1(16^1) + 2(16^0) = 1(16) + 2(1) = 16 + 2 = 18_{10}$$

How many transponders do I ask for?
$$30_{10} = \underline{1E}_{16}$$

Convert using the repeated-division method with 16 as the divisor.

$$
\begin{array}{r}
0 \text{ R } 1 \\
16\overline{)\,1} \text{ R } 14 \\
16\overline{)\,30}
\end{array}
$$

The remainder 14_{10} is equivalent to E_{16}, so $30_{10} = 1E_{16}$.

x	1	2	3	4	5	6	7	8	9	A	B	C	D	E	F	10
1	1	2	3	4	5	6	7	8	9	A	B	C	D	E	F	10
2	2	4	6	8	A	C	E	10	12	14	16	18	1A	1C	1E	20
3	3	6	9	C	F	12	15	18	1B	1E	21	24	27	2A	2D	30
4	4	8	C	10	14	18	1C	20	24	28	2C	30	34	38	3C	40
5	5	A	F	14	19	1E	23	28	2D	32	37	3C	41	46	4B	50
6	6	C	12	18	1E	24	2A	30	36	3C	42	48	4E	54	5A	60
7	7	E	15	1C	23	2A	31	38	3F	46	4D	54	5B	62	69	70
8	8	10	18	20	28	30	38	40	48	50	58	60	68	70	78	80
9	9	12	1B	24	2D	36	3F	48	51	5A	63	6C	75	7E	87	90
A	A	14	1E	28	32	3C	46	50	5A	64	6E	78	82	8C	96	A0
B	B	16	21	2C	37	42	4D	58	63	6E	79	84	8F	9A	A5	B0
C	C	18	24	30	3C	48	54	60	6C	78	84	90	9C	A8	B4	C0
D	D	1A	27	34	41	4E	5B	68	75	82	8F	9C	A9	B6	C3	D0
E	E	1C	2A	38	46	54	62	70	7E	8C	9A	A8	B6	C4	D2	E0
F	F	1E	2D	3C	4B	5A	69	78	87	96	A5	B4	C3	D2	E1	F0
10	10	20	30	40	50	60	70	80	90	A0	B0	C0	D0	E0	F0	100

This problem takes some thought and should be given as an assignment.

Be sure the students are proficient at counting in base 16 before assigning this problem.

How are multiplication facts derived for bases other than 10? Again, examining how it's done for base 10 gives a clue how it is done for another base.

Multiplication is repeated addition. In base 10, multiplying 4 by 8 equals 8 + 8 + 8 + 8. Multiplication facts in any base can found the same way **as long as the addition is done in the desired base.**

Is there a quicker way?

In base 10, counting by 2s gives the multiples of 2.
In base 10, counting by 3s gives the multiples of 3.
In base 10, counting by 4s gives the multiples of 4.

Get the idea?

Count in base 16 from 1_{16} to 100_{16}.

The multiples of 2_{16} will be every second number.
The multiples of 3_{16} will be every third number.

The multiples of E_{16} will be every E_{16}th number.
The multiples of F_{16} will be every F_{16}th number.
The multiples of 10_{16} will be every 10_{16}th number.

The multiples of 2_{16} are in bold and occupy row 2 and column 2 of the multiplication table.

1	**2**	3	**4**	5	**6**	7	**8**	9	**A**	B	**C**	D	**E**	F	**10**
11	**12**	13	**14**	15	**16**	17	18	19	**1A**	1B	**1C**	1D	**1E**	1F	**20**

The multiples of 3_{16} are in bold and occupy row 3 and column 3 of the multiplication table.

1	2	**3**	4	5	**6**	7	8	**9**	A	B	**C**	D	E	**F**	10
11	**12**	13	14	**15**	16	17	**18**	19	1A	**1B**	1C	1D	**1E**	1F	20
21	22	23	**24**	25	26	**27**	28	29	**2A**	2B	2C	**2D**	2E	2F	**30**

The multiples of 4_{16} are in bold and occupy row 4 and column 4 of the multiplication table.

1	2	3	**4**	5	6	7	**8**	9	A	B	**C**	D	E	F	**10**
11	12	13	**14**	15	16	17	**18**	19	1A	1B	**1C**	1D	1E	1F	**20**
21	22	23	**24**	25	26	27	**28**	29	2A	2B	**2C**	2D	2E	2F	**30**
31	32	33	**34**	35	36	37	**38**	39	3A	3B	**3C**	3D	3E	3F	**40**

Keep going. It's really pretty easy!

Note: Although the products in the table are symmetric about the main diagonal, all are given to demonstrate that the commutative property of multiplication (2 x 3 = 3 x 2) still holds for multiplication in other bases.

STARLOG 2300

$$0000_2 \text{ is } 0_{16} \qquad 1000_2 \text{ is } 8_{16}$$
$$0001_2 \text{ is } 1_{16} \qquad 1001_2 \text{ is } 9_{16}$$
$$0010_2 \text{ is } 2_{16} \qquad 1010_2 \text{ is } A_{16}$$
$$0011_2 \text{ is } 3_{16} \qquad 1011_2 \text{ is } B_{16}$$
$$0100_2 \text{ is } 4_{16} \qquad 1100_2 \text{ is } C_{16}$$
$$0101_2 \text{ is } 5_{16} \qquad 1101_2 \text{ is } D_{16}$$
$$0110_2 \text{ is } 6_{16} \qquad 1110_2 \text{ is } E_{16}$$
$$0111_2 \text{ is } 7_{16} \qquad 1111_2 \text{ is } F_{16}$$

Because $2^4 = 16$, four-digit binary numbers are single-digit hexadecimal numbers. More information is given in the *Space Traveler's Training Manual* Answer Key, Starlog 1700 & 1800, problem 4.

$$
\begin{array}{rcl}
0001\ 1110_2 & = & 1E_{16} \\
\underline{x \qquad 1101_2} & = & \underline{x \qquad D_{16}} \\
0001\ 1110 & & \\
0\ 0000\ 0000 & & \\
00\ 0111\ 1000 & & \\
\underline{000\ 1111\ 0000} & & \\
001\ 1000\ 0110_2 & = & 186_{16} \text{ spornks (transponders)}
\end{array}
$$

"How many spornks do I owe?"

BAD_{16} spornks (antimatter detector)

$\underline{+\ 186_{16} \text{ spornks (transponders)}}$

$D33_{16}$ total spornks

To find $D_{16} + 6_{16}$, start at D_{16} and count up 6_{16} units in base 16.

What about a more difficult problem like $B_{16} + D_{16}$? Start at B_{16} and count up D_{16} units in base 16.

B_{16} $\quad C_{16}$ $\quad D_{16}$ $\quad E_{16}$ $\quad F_{16}$ $\quad 10_{16}$ $\quad 11_{16}$ $\quad 12_{16}$ $\quad 13_{16}$ $\quad 14_{16}$ $\quad 15_{16}$ $\quad 16_{16}$ $\quad 17_{16}$ $\quad \mathbf{18_{16}}$
(the count up is 1_{16} $\quad 2_{16}$ $\quad 3_{16}$ $\quad 4_{16}$ $\quad 5_{16}$ $\quad 6_{16}$ $\quad 7_{16}$ $\quad 8_{16}$ $\quad 9_{16}$ $\quad A_{16}$ $\quad B_{16}$ $\quad C_{16}$ $\quad \mathbf{D_{16}}$)

So, $B_{16} + D_{16} = \mathbf{18_{16}}$.

Adding may be done by "making 10_{16}" as described in Starlog 1600 answer key.

The **addition facts for base 16** are summarized in the following addition table.

Base 16 Addition Table

+	1	2	3	4	5	6	7	8	9	A	B	C	D	E	F
1	2	3	4	5	6	7	8	9	A	B	C	D	E	F	10
2		4	5	6	7	8	9	A	B	C	D	E	F	10	11
3			6	7	8	9	A	B	C	D	E	F	10	11	12
4				8	9	A	B	C	D	E	F	10	11	12	13
5					A	B	C	D	E	F	10	11	12	13	14
6						C	D	E	F	10	11	12	13	14	15
7							E	F	10	11	12	13	14	15	16
8								10	11	12	13	14	15	16	17
9									12	13	14	15	16	17	18
A										14	15	16	17	18	19
B											16	17	18	19	1A
C												18	19	1A	1B
D													1A	1B	1C
E														1C	1D
F															1E

```
                              1111 0001 R 100
1111₂ ) 1101 0011 0011₂
                    111 1
                    101 10
                     11 11
                      1 111
                      1 111
                        01 0011
                           1111
                            100
```

STARLOG 2400

$$
1111_2 \overline{) \begin{array}{l} 1111\ 0001.\ 0100\ 0100\ \overline{0100} \\ 1101\ 0011\ 0011.\ 0000\ 0000\ 0000_2 \end{array}}
$$

```
                        1111 0001. 0100 0100 0100
          1111₂ ) 1101 0011 0011. 0000 0000 0000₂
                 111 1
                 101 10
                 11 11
                  1 111
                  1 111
                     01 0011
                        1111
                        100   00
                         11   11
                           100 00
                           11 11
                              100 00
                              11 11
                                 100
```

To round up or round down, that is the question.
If the third hexadecimal place is $\underline{8}_{16}$, I should round up.

How much change should I receive to two hexadecimal places?

$12C.00_{16}$ = 300_{10} roogegs
− $E1.44_{16}$ = roogegs I owe to two hexadecimal places
   $4A.BC_{16}$ = change in roogegs to two hexadecimal places

What is $10_{16} - 4_{16}$? Start at 10_{16} and count **down** 4_{16} units in base sixteen.

$$\mathbf{10_{16}} \quad F_{16} \quad E_{16} \quad D_{16} \quad \mathbf{C_{16}} \qquad\qquad \text{So, } 10_{16} - 4_{16} = \mathbf{C_{16}}.$$

What is $1B_{16} - D_{16}$? Start at $1B_{16}$ and count **down** D_{16} units in base sixteen.

$\mathbf{1B_{16}}$	$1A_{16}$	19_{16}	18_{16}	17_{16}	16_{16}	15_{16}	14_{16}	13_{16}	12_{16}	11_{16}	10_{16}	F_{16}	$\mathbf{E_{16}}$
(the count is	1_{16}	2_{16}	3_{16}	4_{16}	5_{16}	6_{16}	7_{16}	8_{16}	9_{16}	A_{16}	B_{16}	C_{16}	D_{16})

So, $1B_{16} - D_{16} = \mathbf{E_{16}}$

For subtraction, the addition table can be used in reverse. Find $1B_{16}$ in row D_{16} in column E_{16}, the difference.

5_6 **melborp x** 3_6 **snalpf =** 23_6 **melborp**

$(5_6 + 5_6) + 5_6 = 14_6 + 5_6 = 23_6$

x	1	2	3	4	5	10	11	12
1	1	2	3	4	5	10	11	12
2		4	10	12	14	20	22	24
3			13	20	23	30	33	40
4				24	32	40	44	52
5					41	50	55	104
10						100	110	120
11							121	132
12								144

Count from 1_6 to 100_6. Every second number is a multiple of 2_6. Every third number is a multiple of 3_6. Keep going. Use the multiplication table to solve the next two problems.

5_6 **melborp/snalpf**

x 3_6 **snalpf/yeoof**

23_6 **melborp/yeoof**

x 45_6 **yeoof/year**

203

1400

2003_6 **melborp/year**

$$223_6 = \textbf{87}_{10} \textbf{ time warps/year}$$
$$5_2 \overline{)\ 2003_6}$$
$$\underline{14}$$
$$20$$
$$\underline{14}$$
$$23$$
$$\underline{23}$$
$$0$$

Now, wasn't that fun?

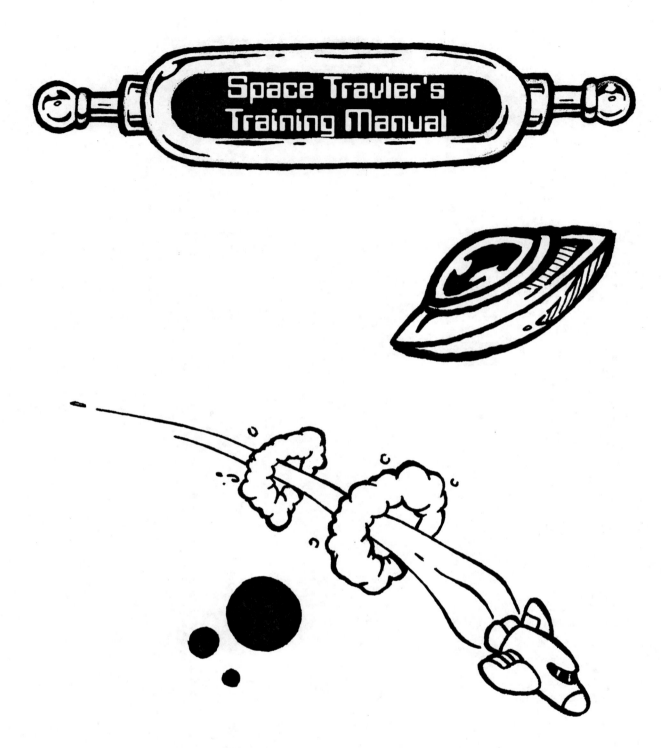

Space Travler's
Training Manual

A problem in "Above & Beyond" is not necessarily difficult, but it does extend beyond the concepts discussed in the corresponding Starlog.

To solve a problem in italic, however, requires insight and critical thinking skills.

STARLOG 1900

1. Count from 37_{10} to 72_{10} in base 6.

37 = _____ $_6$		55 = _____ $_6$
38 = _____ $_6$		56 = _____ $_6$
39 = _____ $_6$		57 = _____ $_6$
40 = _____ $_6$		58 = _____ $_6$
41 = _____ $_6$		59 = _____ $_6$
42 = _____ $_6$		60 = _____ $_6$
43 = _____ $_6$		61 = _____ $_6$
44 = _____ $_6$		62 = _____ $_6$
45 = _____ $_6$		63 = _____ $_6$
46 = _____ $_6$		64 = _____ $_6$
47 = _____ $_6$		65 = _____ $_6$
48 = _____ $_6$		66 = _____ $_6$
49 = _____ $_6$		67 = _____ $_6$
50 = _____ $_6$		68 = _____ $_6$
51 = _____ $_6$		69 = _____ $_6$
52 = _____ $_6$		70 = _____ $_6$
53 = _____ $_6$		71 = _____ $_6$
54 = _____ $_6$		72 = _____ $_6$

2. Count from 1_{10} to 25_{10} in base 5.

1 = _____ $_5$		14 = _____ $_5$
2 = _____ $_5$		15 = _____ $_5$
3 = _____ $_5$		16 = _____ $_5$
4 = _____ $_5$		17 = _____ $_5$
5 = _____ $_5$		18 = _____ $_5$
6 = _____ $_5$		19 = _____ $_5$
7 = _____ $_5$		20 = _____ $_5$
8 = _____ $_5$		21 = _____ $_5$
9 = _____ $_5$		22 = _____ $_5$

$10 = \underline{\hspace{1.5cm}}_5$

$11 = \underline{\hspace{1.5cm}}_5$

$12 = \underline{\hspace{1.5cm}}_5$

$13 = \underline{\hspace{1.5cm}}_5$

$23 = \underline{\hspace{1.5cm}}_5$

$24 = \underline{\hspace{1.5cm}}_5$

$25 = \underline{\hspace{1.5cm}}_5$

3. Convert each of the following numbers to base 10.

(a) $100_8 = \underline{\hspace{1.5cm}}_{10}$

(b) $30_6 = \underline{\hspace{1.5cm}}_{10}$

(c) $1000_4 = \underline{\hspace{1.5cm}}_{10}$

(d) $400_7 = \underline{\hspace{1.5cm}}_{10}$

(e) $300_9 = \underline{\hspace{1.5cm}}_{10}$

(f) $10000_3 = \underline{\hspace{1.5cm}}_{10}$

(g) $1000_7 = \underline{\hspace{1.5cm}}_{10}$

(h) $50_7 = \underline{\hspace{1.5cm}}_{10}$

4. Convert each of the following base 10 numbers to base 6.

(a) $558_{10} = \underline{\hspace{1.5cm}}_6$

(b) $1030_{10} = \underline{\hspace{1.5cm}}_6$

(c) $854_{10} = \underline{\hspace{1.5cm}}_6$

(d) $2981_{10} = \underline{\hspace{1.5cm}}_6$

Above and Beyond

5. *Find another method of converting base 10 numbers to base 6. Repeat problem 4 using your new method to check the method's accuracy and ease of use.*

STARLOG 1500

1. Using the repeated-division method, convert each of the following base 10 numbers to the base indicated.

    (a) $213_{10} = $ _____ $_5$ (b) $89_{10} = $ _____ $_7$

    (c) $65_{10} = $ _____ $_4$ (d) $555_{10} = $ _____ $_6$

    (e) $487_{10} = $ _____ $_9$ (f) $236_{10} = $ _____ $_3$

    (g) $2983_{10} = $ _____ $_8$ (h) $400_{10} = $ _____ $_4$

2. Convert each of the following numbers to base 10.

    (a) $55_8 = $ _____ $_{10}$ (b) $1123_4 = $ _____ $_{10}$

    (c) $1000_5 = $ _____ $_{10}$ (d) $120_7 = $ _____ $_{10}$

    (e) $522_7 = $ _____ $_{10}$ (f) $1030_5 = $ _____ $_{10}$

    (g) $11122_4 = $ _____ $_{10}$ (h) $121_9 = $ _____ $_{10}$

Above and Beyond

3. Convert each of the following fractions to base 10.

(a) $\left(\dfrac{4}{21}\right)_6 = \underline{\hspace{2cm}}_{10}$

(b) $\left(\dfrac{3}{13}\right)_4 = \underline{\hspace{2cm}}_{10}$

(c) $\left(\dfrac{11}{21}\right)_5 = \underline{\hspace{2cm}}_{10}$

(d) $\left(\dfrac{10}{20}\right)_7 = \underline{\hspace{2cm}}_{10}$

(e) $\left(13\dfrac{21}{32}\right)_4 = \underline{\hspace{2cm}}_{10}$

(f) $\left(\dfrac{81}{17}\right)_9 = \underline{\hspace{2cm}}_{10}$

(g) $\left(46\dfrac{16}{37}\right)_8 = \underline{\hspace{2cm}}_{10}$

(h) $\left(\dfrac{41}{12}\right)_3 = \underline{\hspace{2cm}}_{10}$

4. Convert each of the following base 10 fractions to the base indicated.

(a) $\left(\dfrac{1}{6}\right)_{10} = \underline{\hspace{2cm}}_6$

(b) $\left(\dfrac{5}{12}\right)_{10} = \underline{\hspace{2cm}}_6$

(c) $\left(\dfrac{3}{8}\right)_{10} = \underline{\hspace{2cm}}_6$

(d) $\left(\dfrac{11}{36}\right)_{10} = \underline{\hspace{2cm}}_6$

(e) $\left(\dfrac{10}{81}\right)_{10} = \underline{\hspace{2cm}}_9$

(f) $\left(10\dfrac{7}{36}\right)_{10} = \underline{\hspace{2cm}}_4$

(g) $\left(\dfrac{7}{15}\right)_{10} = \underline{\hspace{2cm}}_5$

(h) $\left(\dfrac{17}{9}\right)_{10} = \underline{\hspace{2cm}}_7$

(i) $\left(1\dfrac{8}{9}\right)_{10} = \underline{\hspace{2cm}}_8$

(j) $\left(4\dfrac{5}{11}\right)_{10} = \underline{\hspace{2cm}}_3$

5. Convert each of the following base 6 fractions to a hexamal (same as a decimal except the base is 6).

(a) $\left(\dfrac{103}{1000}\right)_6 = \underline{\hspace{1.5cm}}_6$

(b) $\left(\dfrac{3}{1000}\right)_6 = \underline{\hspace{1.5cm}}_6$

(c) $\left(\dfrac{1153}{10}\right)_6 = \underline{\hspace{1.5cm}}_6$

(d) $\left(\dfrac{52}{10000}\right)_6 = \underline{\hspace{1.5cm}}_6$

(e) $\left(14\dfrac{53}{100}\right)_6 = \underline{\hspace{1.5cm}}_6$

(f) $\left(54\dfrac{22}{10000}\right)_6 = \underline{\hspace{1.5cm}}_6$

STARLOG 1600

1. Find the sum or difference in the base indicated. **Do not convert to base 10 before adding or subtracting.**

(a) 154_6
      $+ 231_6$

(b) 452_6
      $+ 25_6$

(c) 1542_6
      $- 555_6$

(d) 1000_6
      $- 432_6$

(e) 781_9
      $+ 245_9$

(f) 443_5
      $+ 344_5$

(g) 736_8
      $+ 542_8$

(h) 654_7
      $+ 342_7$

(i) 233_4
      $+ 212_4$

(j) 2122_3
      $+ 2121_3$

(k) 2000_5
      $- 431_5$

(l) 7304_8
      $- 621_8$

(m) 5040_9
      $- 876_9$

(n) 3415_7
      $- 666_7$

(o) 3000_4
      $- 233_4$

(p) 1021_3
      $- 222_3$

(q) $7.71_9 + 24.5_9 =$ _____ $_9$

(r) $1.5_8 - 0.736_8 =$ _____ $_8$

(s) $1202_3 - 21.22_3 =$ _____ $_3$

(t) $2.416_7 + 6.66_7 =$ _____ $_7$

STARLOG 1700 & 1800

1. Count from 33_{10} to 64_{10} in base 2. Numbers in base 2 are also known as binary numbers.

33 = _____$_2$	49 = _____$_2$
34 = _____$_2$	50 = _____$_2$
35 = _____$_2$	51 = _____$_2$
36 = _____$_2$	52 = _____$_2$
37 = _____$_2$	53 = _____$_2$
38 = _____$_2$	54 = _____$_2$
39 = _____$_2$	55 = _____$_2$
40 = _____$_2$	56 = _____$_2$
41 = _____$_2$	57 = _____$_2$
42 = _____$_2$	58 = _____$_2$
43 = _____$_2$	59 = _____$_2$
44 = _____$_2$	60 = _____$_2$
45 = _____$_2$	61 = _____$_2$
46 = _____$_2$	62 = _____$_2$
47 = _____$_2$	63 = _____$_2$
48 = _____$_2$	64 = _____$_2$

2. Convert the following binary numbers to base 10.

(a) 1010101_2 = _____$_{10}$

(b) 100000000_2 = _____$_{10}$

(c) 111111111_2 = _____$_{10}$

(d) 110100111_2 = _____$_{10}$

Above and Beyond

3. Convert each of the following binary numbers to a fraction in base 10.

   (a) 101.11_2 = _____$_{10}$

   (b) 10101.001_2 = _____$_{10}$

   (c) 0.10011_2 = _____$_{10}$

   (d) 100011.1011_2 = _____$_{10}$

4. *Convert each of the following binary numbers to base indicated **without using base 10 as an intermediate step.***

   (a) 11011011_2 = _____$_4$

   (b) 1001001_2 = _____$_4$

   (c) 111110_2 = _____$_8$

   (d) 11001011_2 = _____$_8$

STARLOG 1900

1. Using the repeated-division method, convert each of the following base 10 numbers to binary.

    (a) $71_{10} = $ _____$_2$

    (b) $84_{10} = $ _____$_2$

    (c) $196_{10} = $ _____$_2$

    (d) $750_{10} = $ _____$_2$

    (e) $300_{10} = $ _____$_2$

    (f) $163_{10} = $ _____$_2$

    (g) $1012_{10} = $ _____$_2$

    (h) $295_{10} = $ _____$_2$

Above and Beyond

2. Convert each of the following base 10 fractions to binary.

    (a) $\left(11\frac{3}{7}\right)_{10} = $ _____$_2$

    (b) $\left(\frac{6}{11}\right)_{10} = $ _____$_2$

    (c) $\left(2\frac{3}{14}\right)_{10} = $ _____$_2$

    (b) $\left(\frac{19}{32}\right)_{10} = $ _____$_2$

3. **_Without using base 10 as an intermediate step_**, *convert each of the following binary numbers to base 5. (Hint: What are* 1_2, 10_2, 100_2, *..., equivalent to in base 5?)*

    (a) $10010_2 =$ _____$_5$ (b) $11101_2 =$ _____$_5$

    (c) $101111_2 =$ _____$_5$ (d) $1101_2 =$ _____$_5$

4. **_Without using base 10 as an intermediate step_**, *convert each of the following base 3 numbers to base 7. (Hint: What are* 1_3, 10_3, 100_3, *..., equivalent to in base 7?)*

    (a) $12011_3 =$ _____$_7$ (b) $12201_3 =$ _____$_7$

    (c) $201210_3 =$ _____$_7$ (d) $1222_3 =$ _____$_7$

STARLOG 2000 & 2100

1. Perform the indicated operation. The exponents are in base 10 for clarity and to avoid subscripting an exponent.

(a) 10100111_2
$+ \ \ 1110111_2$

(b) 1100110011_2
$+ 1111000011_2$

(c) 10111101_2
$- \ \ 1001101_2$

(d) 10010000_2
$- \ \ \ \ 110011_2$

(e) 10001000_2
$- \ \ 1111111_2$

(f) 100111001_2
$- 100010011_2$

(g) 10111_2
$\text{x} \ \ 1010_2$

(h) 1101011_2
$\text{x} \ \ \ \ \ 1111_2$

(i) $(11011_2)^3 \ = \ $ _____$_2$

(j) $(1000_2)^4 \ = \ $ _____$_2$

(k) $(111000010_2) \div (110_2) \ = \ $ _____$_2$

(l) $(11111100_2) \div (1001_2) \ = \ $ _____$_2$

Above and Beyond

2. Convert each of the following binary fractions to a bimal (same as a decimal except the base is 2).

(a) $\left(\dfrac{1}{11}\right)_2 = \underline{\hspace{2cm}}_2$

(b) $\left(\dfrac{111}{11100}\right)_2 = \underline{\hspace{2cm}}_2$

(c) $\left(\dfrac{11}{111}\right)_2 = \underline{\hspace{2cm}}_2$

(d) $\left(\dfrac{10101}{10101000}\right)_2 = \underline{\hspace{2cm}}_2$

(e) $\left(\dfrac{10}{101}\right)_2 = \underline{\hspace{2cm}}_2$

(f) $\left(\dfrac{1001}{11000}\right)_2 = \underline{\hspace{2cm}}_2$

3. **Without using base 10 as an intermediate step**, reduce the following binary fractions.

(a) $\left(\dfrac{10010}{100100}\right)_2 = \underline{\hspace{2cm}}_2$

(b) $\left(\dfrac{11000}{100000}\right)_2 = \underline{\hspace{2cm}}_2$

(c) $\left(\dfrac{11}{10010}\right)_2 = \underline{\hspace{2cm}}_2$

(d) $\left(\dfrac{111}{100011}\right)_2 = \underline{\hspace{2cm}}_2$

(e) $\left(\dfrac{1010}{1111}\right)_2 = \underline{\hspace{2cm}}_2$

(f) $\left(\dfrac{1100}{100000}\right)_2 = \underline{\hspace{2cm}}_2$

4. **Without using base 10 as an intermediate step**, perform the indicated operations expressing each answer as a binary fraction in **lowest terms**.

(a) $\left(\dfrac{11}{1000}\right)_2 \times \left(\dfrac{100}{101}\right)_2$

(b) $\left(\dfrac{1}{11}\right)_2 \times \left(\dfrac{110}{111}\right)_2$

(c) $\left(\dfrac{11}{1011}\right)_2 \times \left(\dfrac{10110}{1001}\right)_2$

(d) $\left(\dfrac{110}{111}\right)_2 \times \left(\dfrac{1110}{1111}\right)_2$

(e) $\left(\dfrac{101}{1110}\right)_2 \div \left(\dfrac{1111}{111}\right)_2$

(f) $\left(\dfrac{11}{100}\right)_2 \div \left(\dfrac{101}{1100}\right)_2$

(g) $\left(\dfrac{11}{100}\right)_2 + \left(\dfrac{11}{1000}\right)_2$

(h) $\left(\dfrac{11}{101}\right)_2 + \left(\dfrac{100}{1111}\right)_2$

(i) $\left(\dfrac{111}{10010}\right)_2 - \left(\dfrac{10}{1001}\right)_2$

(j) $\left(\dfrac{101}{1001}\right)_2 - \left(\dfrac{10}{111}\right)_2$

STARLOG 2200

1. Convert each of the following numbers to base 10.

   (a) $A55_{12}$ = _____ $_{10}$ (b) $1C3_{15}$ = _____ $_{10}$

   (c) $2FG_{17}$ = _____ $_{10}$ (d) BED_{16} = _____ $_{10}$

   (e) ABC_{14} = _____ $_{10}$ (f) $H5D_{20}$ = _____ $_{10}$

   (g) $8CA_{13}$ = _____ $_{10}$ (h) $G35_{20}$ = _____ $_{10}$

2. Using the repeated-division method, convert each of the following base 10 numbers to the base indicated. When necessary, use letters for additional symbols.

   (a) 213_{10} = _____ $_{12}$ (b) 389_{10} = _____ $_{17}$

   (c) 615_{10} = _____ $_{15}$ (d) 555_{10} = _____ $_{18}$

   (e) 487_{10} = _____ $_{13}$ (f) 236_{10} = _____ $_{11}$

   (g) 2983_{10} = _____ $_{20}$ (h) 400_{10} = _____ $_{19}$

3. Make the multiplication table for base 12.

STARLOG 2300 & 2900

1. Perform the indicated operation **using binary as an intermediate step**.

(a) 113_4
       $\text{x}\;\;\;22_4$

(b) 1223_4
       $\text{x}\;\;\;33_4$

(c) 153_8
       $\text{x}\;\;\;17_8$

(d) 27_8
       $\text{x}\;\;\;12_8$

(e) $(13002_4) \div (12_4) \;\; = \;\; \underline{\hspace{2cm}}_4$

(f) $(3330_4) \div (21_4) \;\; = \;\; \underline{\hspace{2cm}}_4$

(g) $(702_8) \div (6_8) \;\; = \;\; \underline{\hspace{2cm}}_8$

(h) $(6631_8) \div (73_8) \;\; = \;\; \underline{\hspace{2cm}}_8$

2. Find the sum or difference in the base indicated. **Do not convert to base 10 before adding or subtracting.**

(a) $8B5_{16}$
     $+ A7C_{16}$

(b) $479C_{16}$
     $+ 8ED_{16}$

(c) FAD_{16}
     $+ CAB_{16}$

(d) ABC_{14}
     $+ 754_{14}$

(e) BDE_{17}
     $+ 3GF_{17}$

(f) $D5H_{20}$
     $+ IDC_{20}$

(g) 1321_{16}
     $- A7C_{16}$

(h) FAB_{16}
     $- CAD_{16}$

(i) $3B95_{16}$
     $- 6CF_{16}$

Above and Beyond

3. Convert each of the following numbers to the base indicated **without using base 10 as an intermediate step.**

(a) 31323_4 = _____$_{16}$

(b) 213011_4 = _____$_{16}$

(c) $C6E_{16}$ = _____$_4$

(d) FC_{16} = _____$_4$

(e) 21221_3 = _____$_9$

(f) 112201_3 = _____$_9$

(g) 586_9 = _____$_3$

(h) 148_9 = _____$_3$

STARLOG 2500

1. Make the multiplication table for base 7.

2. Find the products.

(a) 542_6
   $\times\ 34_6$

(b) 44.44_6
   $\times\ 35.2_6$

(c) 503.4_6
   $\times\ .234_6$

3. Find the quotients to two hexamal places.

   (a) $(4212_6) \div (0.5_6)$ = _____ $_6$

   (b) $(5334_6) \div (12_6)$ = _____ $_6$

   (c) $(4.325_6) \div (1.4_6)$ = _____ $_6$

Above and Beyond

4. Convert each of the following base 6 fractions to a hexamal (same as a decimal except the base is 6).

(a) $\left(\dfrac{3}{4}\right)_6$ = _____ $_6$

(b) $\left(\dfrac{13}{14}\right)_6$ = _____ $_6$

(c) $\left(\dfrac{1}{2}\right)_6$ = _____ $_6$

(d) $\left(\dfrac{3}{5}\right)_6$ = _____ $_6$

5. State the divisibility rules for 2, 3, 4, and 5 in base 6.

6. Convert each of the following hexamals to a base 6 fraction **in lowest terms**.

(a) 21.003_6 = _____ $_6$ = _____ $_6$
     (mixed)   (improper)

(b) 521.014_6 = _____ $_6$ = _____ $_6$
      (mixed)   (improper)

(c) 0.504_6 = _____ $_6$

(d) 0.0024453_6 = _____ $_6$

7. **Without using base 10 as an intermediate step**, perform the indicated operations expressing each answer as a base 6 fraction **in lowest terms**.

(a) $\left(\dfrac{3}{12}\right)_6$ x $\left(\dfrac{4}{5}\right)_6$

(b) $\left(\dfrac{1}{3}\right)_6$ x $\left(\dfrac{10}{11}\right)_6$

(c) $\left(\dfrac{10}{55}\right)_6$ x $\left(\dfrac{200}{23}\right)_6$

(d) $\left(\dfrac{5}{100}\right)_6$ x $\left(\dfrac{41}{13}\right)_6$

(e) $\left(\dfrac{3}{5}\right)_6$ ÷ $\left(\dfrac{20}{23}\right)_6$

(f) $\left(\dfrac{4}{11}\right)_6$ ÷ $\left(\dfrac{20}{11}\right)_6$

(g) $\left(\dfrac{3}{4}\right)_6$ + $\left(\dfrac{3}{12}\right)_6$

(h) $\left(\dfrac{3}{5}\right)_6$ + $\left(\dfrac{4}{23}\right)_6$

(i) $\left(\dfrac{11}{30}\right)_6$ − $\left(\dfrac{2}{13}\right)_6$

(j) $\left(\dfrac{5}{13}\right)_6$ − $\left(\dfrac{2}{11}\right)_6$

Training Manual
Answer Key

STARLOG 1900

1. Count from 37_{10} to 72_{10} in base 6.

37 = $\underline{101}_6$	55 = $\underline{131}_6$
38 = $\underline{102}_6$	56 = $\underline{132}_6$
39 = $\underline{103}_6$	57 = $\underline{133}_6$
40 = $\underline{104}_6$	58 = $\underline{134}_6$
41 = $\underline{105}_6$	59 = $\underline{135}_6$
42 = $\underline{110}_6$	60 = $\underline{140}_6$
43 = $\underline{111}_6$	61 = $\underline{141}_6$
44 = $\underline{112}_6$	62 = $\underline{142}_6$
45 = $\underline{113}_6$	63 = $\underline{143}_6$
46 = $\underline{114}_6$	64 = $\underline{144}_6$
47 = $\underline{115}_6$	65 = $\underline{145}_6$
48 = $\underline{120}_6$	66 = $\underline{150}_6$
49 = $\underline{121}_6$	67 = $\underline{151}_6$
50 = $\underline{122}_6$	68 = $\underline{152}_6$
51 = $\underline{123}_6$	69 = $\underline{153}_6$
52 = $\underline{124}_6$	70 = $\underline{154}_6$
53 = $\underline{125}_6$	71 = $\underline{155}_6$
54 = $\underline{130}_6$	72 = $\underline{200}_6$

2. Count from 1_{10} to 25_{10} in base 5.

1 = $\underline{1}_5$	14 = $\underline{24}_5$
2 = $\underline{2}_5$	15 = $\underline{30}_5$
3 = $\underline{3}_5$	16 = $\underline{31}_5$
4 = $\underline{4}_5$	17 = $\underline{32}_5$
5 = $\underline{10}_5$	18 = $\underline{33}_5$
6 = $\underline{11}_5$	19 = $\underline{34}_5$
7 = $\underline{12}_5$	20 = $\underline{40}_5$
8 = $\underline{13}_5$	21 = $\underline{41}_5$
9 = $\underline{14}_5$	22 = $\underline{42}_5$
10 = $\underline{15}_5$	23 = $\underline{43}_5$

$$11 = \underline{21}_5 \qquad\qquad 24 = \underline{44}_5$$
$$12 = \underline{22}_5 \qquad\qquad 25 = \underline{100}_5$$
$$13 = \underline{23}_5$$

3. Convert each of the following numbers to base 10.

(a) $100_8 = 8^2 \qquad = \mathbf{\underline{64}}_{10}$ (b) $30_6 = 3 \times 6^1 \qquad = \mathbf{\underline{18}}_{10}$

(c) $1000_4 = 4^3 \qquad = \mathbf{\underline{64}}_{10}$ (d) $400_7 = 4 \times 7^2 \quad = \mathbf{\underline{196}}_{10}$

(e) $300_9 = 3 \times 9^2 = \mathbf{\underline{243}}_{10}$ (f) $10000_3 = 3^4 \qquad\quad = \mathbf{\underline{81}}_{10}$

(g) $1000_7 = 7^3 \qquad = \mathbf{\underline{343}}_{10}$ (h) $50_7 = 5 \times 7^1 \qquad = \mathbf{\underline{35}}_{10}$

The place-value occupied by any digit is a power of the base, but what power? The power of the base is the number of digits following the place-value. For (d), 4 is in the 49th place (the *second* power of 7) because two digits follow 4.

4. Convert each of the following base 10 numbers to base 6.

(a) $558_{10} = \mathbf{\underline{2330}}_6$

(b) $1030_{10} = \mathbf{\underline{4434}}_6$

(c) $854_{10} = \mathbf{\underline{3542}}_6$

(d) $2981_{10} = \mathbf{\underline{21445}}_6$

Refer to Starlog 1400 answer key.

Above and Beyond

5. *Find another method of converting base 10 numbers to base. Repeat problem 4 using your new method to check the method's accuracy and ease of use.*

Refer to Starlog 1400 answer key, the repeated-division method.

STARLOG 1500

1. Using the repeated-division method, convert each of the following base 10 numbers to the base indicated.

   (a) 213_{10} = $\underline{1323}_5$ (b) 89_{10} = $\underline{155}_7$

   (c) 65_{10} = $\underline{1001}_4$ (d) 555_{10} = $\underline{2323}_6$

   (e) 487_{10} = $\underline{601}_9$ (f) 236_{10} = $\underline{22202}_3$

   (g) 2983_{10} = $\underline{5647}_8$ (h) 400_{10} = $\underline{12100}_4$

Refer to Starlog 1400 answer key, <u>the repeated-division method</u>. The base 10 number is divided repeatedly by the base indicated.

2. Convert each of the following numbers to base 10.

   (a) 55_8 = $\underline{45}_{10}$ (b) 1123_4 = $\underline{91}_{10}$

   (c) 1000_5 = $\underline{125}_{10}$ (d) 120_7 = $\underline{63}_{10}$

   (e) 522_7 = $\underline{261}_{10}$ (f) 1030_5 = $\underline{140}_{10}$

   (g) 11122_4 = $\underline{346}_{10}$ (h) 121_9 = $\underline{100}_{10}$

Refer to Starlog 1500 answer key. Change the base from 6 to the current base.

Above and Beyond

3. Convert each of the following fractions to base 10.

(a) $\left(\dfrac{4}{21}\right)_6 = \left(\dfrac{4}{13}\right)_{10}$

(b) $\left(\dfrac{3}{13}\right)_4 = \left(\dfrac{3}{7}\right)_{10}$

(c) $\left(\dfrac{11}{21}\right)_5 = \left(\dfrac{6}{11}\right)_{10}$

(d) $\left(\dfrac{10}{20}\right)_7 = \left(\dfrac{1}{2}\right)_{10}$

(e) $\left(13\dfrac{21}{32}\right)_4 = \left(7\dfrac{9}{14}\right)_{10}$

(f) $\left(\dfrac{81}{17}\right)_9 = \left(\dfrac{73}{16}\right)$ or $\left(4\dfrac{9}{16}\right)_{10}$

(g) $\left(46\dfrac{16}{37}\right)_8 = \left(38\dfrac{14}{31}\right)_{10}$

(h) $\left(\dfrac{41}{12}\right)_3 = \left(\dfrac{13}{5}\right)$ or $\left(2\dfrac{3}{5}\right)_{10}$

Whether a number is the whole part, numerator, or denominator, it must be converted to base 10.

4. Convert each of the following base 10 fractions to the base indicated.

(a) $\left(\dfrac{1}{6}\right)_{10} = \left(\dfrac{1}{10}\right)_{6}$

(b) $\left(\dfrac{5}{12}\right)_{10} = \left(\dfrac{5}{20}\right)_{6}$

(c) $\left(\dfrac{3}{8}\right)_{10} = \left(\dfrac{3}{12}\right)_{6}$

(d) $\left(\dfrac{11}{36}\right)_{10} = \left(\dfrac{15}{100}\right)_{6}$

(e) $\left(\dfrac{10}{81}\right)_{10} = \left(\dfrac{11}{100}\right)_{9}$

(f) $\left(10\dfrac{7}{36}\right)_{10} = \left(22\dfrac{13}{210}\right)_{4}$

(g) $\left(\dfrac{7}{15}\right)_{10} = \left(\dfrac{12}{30}\right)_{5}$

(h) $\left(\dfrac{17}{9}\right)_{10} = \left(\dfrac{23}{12}\right) \text{ or } \left(1\dfrac{11}{12}\right)_{7}$

(i) $\left(1\dfrac{8}{9}\right)_{10} = \left(1\dfrac{10}{11}\right)_{8}$

(j) $\left(4\dfrac{5}{11}\right)_{10} = \left(11\dfrac{12}{102}\right)_{3}$

Whether a number is the whole part, numerator, or denominator, it must be converted to base 10.

Notice each denominator in (a), (d), and (e) is a power of the desired base. The new denominator is always a one followed by a number of zeroes equal to the power of the desired base.

5. Convert each of the following base 6 fractions to a hexamal (same as a decimal except the base is 6).

(a) $\left(\dfrac{103}{1000}\right)_6$ = **0.103**$_6$ (b) $\left(\dfrac{3}{1000}\right)_6$ = **0.003**$_6$

(c) $\left(\dfrac{1153}{10}\right)_6$ = **115.3**$_6$ (d) $\left(\dfrac{52}{10000}\right)_6$ = **0.0052**$_6$

(e) $\left(14\dfrac{53}{100}\right)_6$ = **14.53**$_6$ (f) $\left(54\dfrac{22}{10000}\right)_6$ = **54.0022**$_6$

Converting fractions to decimals is exactly the same as converting fractions to hexamals except the base is 6.

STARLOG 1600

1. Find the sum or difference in the base indicated. **Do not convert to base 10 before adding or subtracting.**

(a) $\begin{array}{r} 154_6 \\ + 231_6 \\ \hline \mathbf{425_6} \end{array}$
(b) $\begin{array}{r} 452_6 \\ + 25_6 \\ \hline \mathbf{521_6} \end{array}$
(c) $\begin{array}{r} 1542_6 \\ - 555_6 \\ \hline \mathbf{543_6} \end{array}$
(d) $\begin{array}{r} 1000_6 \\ - 432_6 \\ \hline \mathbf{124_6} \end{array}$

(e) $\begin{array}{r} 781_9 \\ + 245_9 \\ \hline \mathbf{1136_9} \end{array}$
(f) $\begin{array}{r} 443_5 \\ + 344_5 \\ \hline \mathbf{1342_5} \end{array}$
(g) $\begin{array}{r} 736_8 \\ + 542_8 \\ \hline \mathbf{1500_8} \end{array}$
(h) $\begin{array}{r} 654_7 \\ + 342_7 \\ \hline \mathbf{1326_7} \end{array}$

(i) $\begin{array}{r} 233_4 \\ + 212_4 \\ \hline \mathbf{1111_4} \end{array}$
(j) $\begin{array}{r} 2122_3 \\ + 2121_3 \\ \hline \mathbf{12020_3} \end{array}$
(k) $\begin{array}{r} 2000_5 \\ - 431_5 \\ \hline \mathbf{1014_5} \end{array}$
(l) $\begin{array}{r} 7304_8 \\ - 621_8 \\ \hline \mathbf{6463_8} \end{array}$

(m) $\begin{array}{r} 5040_9 \\ - 876_9 \\ \hline \mathbf{4053_9} \end{array}$
(n) $\begin{array}{r} 3415_7 \\ - 666_7 \\ \hline \mathbf{2416_7} \end{array}$
(o) $\begin{array}{r} 3000_4 \\ - 233_4 \\ \hline \mathbf{2101_4} \end{array}$
(p) $\begin{array}{r} 1021_3 \\ - 222_3 \\ \hline \mathbf{22_3} \end{array}$

(q) $7.71_9 + 24.5_9 \quad = \quad \mathbf{\underline{33.31_9}}$

(r) $1.5_8 - 0.736_8 \quad = \quad \mathbf{\underline{0.542_8}}$

(s) $1202_3 - 21.22_3 \quad = \quad \mathbf{\underline{1110.01_3}}$

(t) $2.416_7 + 6.66_7 \quad = \quad \mathbf{\underline{12.406_7}}$

Refer to Starlog 1600 answer key.

STARLOG 1700 & 1800

1. Count from 33_{10} to 64_{10} in base 2. Numbers in base 2 are also known as binary numbers.

33 =	**100001**$_2$		49 =	**110001**$_2$
34 =	**100010**$_2$		50 =	**110010**$_2$
35 =	**100011**$_2$		51 =	**110011**$_2$
36 =	**100100**$_2$		52 =	**110100**$_2$
37 =	**100101**$_2$		53 =	**110101**$_2$
38 =	**100110**$_2$		54 =	**110110**$_2$
39 =	**100111**$_2$		55 =	**110111**$_2$
40 =	**101000**$_2$		56 =	**111000**$_2$
41 =	**101001**$_2$		57 =	**111001**$_2$
42 =	**101010**$_2$		58 =	**111010**$_2$
43 =	**101011**$_2$		59 =	**111011**$_2$
44 =	**101100**$_2$		60 =	**111100**$_2$
45 =	**101101**$_2$		61 =	**111101**$_2$
46 =	**101110**$_2$		62 =	**111110**$_2$
47 =	**101111**$_2$		63 =	**111111**$_2$
48 =	**110000**$_2$		64 =	**1000000**$_2$

2. Convert the following binary numbers to base 10.

   (a) 1010101_2 = **85**$_{10}$

   (b) 100000000_2 = **256**$_{10}$

   (c) 111111111_2 = **511**$_{10}$

   (d) 110100111_2 = **423**$_{10}$

Refer to Starlog 1800 answer key.

Above and Beyond

3. Convert each of the following binary numbers to a fraction in base 10.

(a) 101.11_2 = $\left(101\frac{11}{100}\right)_2$ = $\left(5\frac{3}{4}\right)_{10}$

(b) 10101.001_2 = $\left(10101\frac{1}{1000}\right)_2$ = $\left(21\frac{1}{8}\right)_{10}$

(c) 0.10011_2 = $\left(\frac{10011}{100000}\right)_2$ = $\left(\frac{19}{32}\right)_{10}$

(d) 100011.1011_2 = $\left(100011\frac{1011}{10000}\right)_2$ = $\left(35\frac{11}{16}\right)_{10}$

First, convert each binary number to a binary fraction. Next, convert each number in the binary fraction to base 10.

Space Traveler's Training Manual Answer Key

4. ***Without using base 10 as an intermediate step***, *convert each of the following binary numbers to the base indicated.*

(a) 11011011_2 =   **3123**$_4$

(b) 1001001_2 =   **1021**$_4$

(c) 111110_2 =   **76**$_8$

(d) 11001011_2 =   **313**$_8$

This problem introduces a very important concept discussed in Starlog 2300.

Consider the desired bases 4 and 8. Both of these bases are powers of 2. Is it possible to use that fact to convert binary numbers directly to base 4 and base 8 without converting to base 10? Most definitely!

Since 4 is the second power of 2, <u>separate the binary number into *two-digit* binary numbers and convert each of the two-digit binary numbers to base 4</u> resulting in the following:

(a) 11011011_2 = 11_2 01_2 10_2 11_2

        =   **3**   **1**   **2**   **3**$_4$

(b) 1001001_2 = 1_2 00_2 10_2 01_2

        =   **1**   **0**   **2**   **1**$_4$

What a slick solution! Separating into two-digit binary numbers ensures that the only symbols in the base 4 equivalent will be 0, 1, 2, or 3, the only digits occurring in base 4.

Is the solution correct? To check the answer, convert both the original binary number to base 10 and the base 4 equivalent to base 10. Both should be the same answer. For (a), both 11011011_2 and 3123_4 are equivalent to 219_{10}. For (b), both 1001001_2 and 1021_4 are equivalent to 73_{10}.

What about base 8? Since 8 is the *third* power of 2, separate the binary number into *three-digit* binary numbers and convert each of the three-digit binary numbers to base 8. Let's try (c) and (d).

(c)	$111110_2 =$	111_2	110_2	
	$=$	7	6_8	

(c)	$11001011_2 =$	11_2	001_2	011_2
	$=$	3	1	3_8

Separating into three-digit binary numbers ensures that the only symbols in the base 8 equivalent will be 0, 1, 2, 3, 4, 5, 6, or 7, the only digits occurring in base 8.

Is the solution correct? For (c), both 111110_2 and 76_8 are equivalent to 62_{10}. For (d), both 11001011_2 and 313_8 are equivalent to 203_{10}.

STARLOG 1900

1. Using the repeated-division method, convert each of the following base 10 numbers to binary.

   (a) 71_{10} = **1000111_2** (b) 84_{10} = **1010100_2**

   (c) 196_{10} = **11000100_2** (d) 750_{10} = **1011101110_2**

   (e) 300_{10} = **100101100_2** (f) 163_{10} = **10100011_2**

   (g) 1012_{10} = **1111110100_2** (h) 295_{10} = **100100111_2**

Refer to Starlog 1400 answer key, the repeated-division method. Divide repeatedly by 2, the desired base.

Above and Beyond

2. Convert each of the following base 10 fractions to binary.

   (a) $\left(11\frac{3}{7}\right)_{10} = \left(1011\frac{11}{111}\right)_2$ (b) $\left(\frac{6}{11}\right)_{10} = \left(\frac{110}{1011}\right)_2$

   (c) $\left(2\frac{3}{14}\right)_{10} = \left(10\frac{11}{1110}\right)_2$ (d) $\left(\frac{19}{32}\right)_{10} = \left(\frac{10011}{100000}\right)_2$

Whether the number is the whole part, numerator, or denominator, it must be converted to binary.

3. ***Without using base 10 as an intermediate step***, *convert each of the following binary numbers to base 5. (Hint: What are 1_2, 10_2, 100_2, ..., equivalent to in base 5?)*

(a) 10010_2 = **33**$_5$

(b) 11101_2 = **104**$_5$

(c) 101111_2 = **142**$_5$

(d) 1101_2 = **23**$_5$

Problems 3 and 4 are closely related and are without a doubt the most challenging so far. Students who arrive at the solution for 3 will probably solve problem 4 as well. Any student who solves both of these problems truly excels at critical thinking and definitely deserves some serious extra-credit points.

Answers with no explanation should not be accepted.

It is natural for students to think in terms of base 10, and they may mentally use base 10 as an intermediate step. That would be too easy! Therefore, <u>do not accept any answers or explanations that mention the numbers 8 or 16 since these numbers exist in base 10, but do not exist in base 5</u>.

The base 10 equivalents for each binary place-value is needed to convert binary to base 10. What are the binary place-values equivalent to in base 5? Only the first six place-values are needed since a six-digit binary number is the largest number to be converted to base 5. In other words, solve the following:

$$1_2 \ = \ \underline{\hspace{1.5cm}}_5$$

$$10_2 \ = \ \underline{\hspace{1.5cm}}_5$$

$$100_2 \ = \ \underline{\hspace{1.5cm}}_5$$

$$1000_2 \ = \ \underline{\hspace{1.5cm}}_5$$

$$10000_2 \ = \ \underline{\hspace{1.5cm}}_5$$

$$100000_2 \ = \ \underline{\hspace{1.5cm}}_5$$

Space Traveler's Training Manual Answer Key

The first three are easy.

$$1_2 = \mathbf{1}_5$$
$$10_2 = \mathbf{2}_5$$
$$100_2 = \mathbf{4}_5$$

Now what? First, realize that in binary, <u>the next higher place-value is simply a double of the lower place-value</u>. So far, multiplying in another base has not been discussed, but remember that multiplication is repeated addition. <u>To find the double, simply add the lower place-value to itself</u>. Second, since the new base is 5, <u>add in base 5</u>.

Base 5 equivalents of binary place-values are in italic.

$$
\begin{array}{rr}
1_2 = & \mathbf{1}_5 \\
 & +\ \ \mathbf{1}_5 \\
\hline
10_2 = & \mathbf{2}_5 \\
 & +\ \ \mathbf{2}_5 \\
\hline
100_2 = & \mathbf{4}_5 \\
 & +\ \ \mathbf{4}_5 \\
\hline
1000_2 = & \mathbf{13}_5 \\
 & +\ \ \mathbf{13}_5 \\
\hline
10000_2 = & \mathbf{31}_5 \\
 & +\ \ \mathbf{31}_5 \\
\hline
100000_2 = & \mathbf{112}_5 \\
 & +\ \ \mathbf{112}_5 \\
\hline
1000000_2 = & \mathbf{224}_5 \\
\end{array}
$$

The process is infinite. Finish recording the base 5 equivalents of the binary place-values.

$$
\begin{array}{rcl}
1000_2 & = & \underline{\mathbf{13}}_5 \\
10000_2 & = & \underline{\mathbf{31}}_5 \\
100000_2 & = & \underline{\mathbf{112}}_5 \\
\end{array}
$$

Space Traveler's Training Manual Answer Key

The conversion from binary to base 5 is completed by adding the equivalent place-values together as follows:

(a) $10010_2 = 31_5 + 2_5 = 33_5$

(b) $11101_2 = 31_5 + 13_5 + 4_5 + 1_5 = 104_5$

(c) $101111_2 = 112_5 + 13_5 + 4_5 + 2_5 + 1_5 = 142_5$

(d) $1101_2 = 13_5 + 4_5 + 1_5 = 23_5$

To check the answer, convert both the binary number and the base 5 equivalent to base 10. Are they the same?

For (a), both 10010_2 and 33_5 are equivalent to 18_{10}.
For (b), both 11101_2 and 104_5 are equivalent to 29_{10}.
For (c), both 101111_2 and 142_5 are equivalent to 47_{10}.
For (d), both 1101_2 and 23_5 are equivalent to 13_{10}.

4. ***Without using base 10 as an intermediate step***, *convert each of the following base 3 numbers to base 7. (Hint: What are 1_3, 10_3, 100_3, ..., equivalent to in base 7?)*

(a) $12011_3 = $ **256_7**   (b) $12201_3 = $ **310_7**

(c) $201210_3 = $ **1362_7**   (d) $1222_3 = $ **104_7**

Any students unable to solve problem 3? Let them have another try at problem 4 after reading the explanation for problem 3.

Since problem 4 is an extension of problem 3, answers with no explanations are still unacceptable.

To convert base 3 to base 7, solve the following:

$$1_3 = \underline{\hspace{1.5cm}}_7$$
$$10_3 = \underline{\hspace{1.5cm}}_7$$
$$100_3 = \underline{\hspace{1.5cm}}_7$$
$$1000_3 = \underline{\hspace{1.5cm}}_7$$
$$10000_3 = \underline{\hspace{1.5cm}}_7$$
$$100000_3 = \underline{\hspace{1.5cm}}_7$$

This solution is similar to the previous problem except <u>the next higher place-value in base 3 is the *triple* of the lower place-value.</u> To find the triple, <u>add the lower place-value to itself *three times*</u>. Since the new base is 7, <u>add in base 7</u>.

Base 7 equivalents of base 3 place-values are in italic.

$$
\begin{aligned}
1_3 = \quad & 1_7\\
& 1_7\\
+\ & 1_7\\
\hline
10_3 = \quad & 3_7\\
& 3_7\\
+\ & 3_7\\
\hline
100_3 = \quad & 12_7\\
& 12_7\\
+\ & 12_7\\
\hline
1000_3 = \quad & 36_7\\
& 36_7\\
+\ & 36_7\\
\hline
10000_3 = \quad & 144_7\\
& 144_7\\
+\ & 144_7\\
\hline
100000_3 = \quad & 465_7
\end{aligned}
$$

Again, the process is infinite. The base 7 equivalents of base 3 place-values are recorded.

$$1_3 = \underline{\mathbf{1}}_7$$
$$10_3 = \underline{\mathbf{3}}_7$$
$$100_3 = \underline{\mathbf{12}}_7$$
$$1000_3 = \underline{\mathbf{36}}_7$$
$$10000_3 = \underline{\mathbf{144}}_7$$
$$100000_3 = \underline{\mathbf{465}}_7$$

The conversion from base 3 to base 7 is completed by adding the equivalent place-values together. <u>Whenever a 2 occupies a place-value in base 3, remember to add the place-value *twice*.</u>

(a) $12011_3 = \mathbf{144}_7 + \mathbf{36}_7 + \mathbf{36}_7 + \mathbf{3}_7 + \mathbf{1}_7 = \mathbf{256}_7$

(b) $12201_3 = \mathbf{144}_7 + \mathbf{36}_7 + \mathbf{36}_7 + \mathbf{12}_7 + \mathbf{12}_7 + \mathbf{1}_7 = \mathbf{310}_7$

(c) $201210_3 = \mathbf{465}_7 + \mathbf{465}_7 + \mathbf{36}_7 + \mathbf{12}_7 + \mathbf{12}_7 + \mathbf{3}_7 = \mathbf{1362}_7$

(d) $1222_3 = \mathbf{36}_7 + \mathbf{12}_7 + \mathbf{12}_7 + \mathbf{3}_7 + \mathbf{3}_7 + \mathbf{1}_7 + \mathbf{1}_7 = \mathbf{104}_7$

Check the answers.

For (a), both 12011_3 and 256_7 are equivalent to 139_{10}.
For (b), both 12201_3 and 310_7 are equivalent to 154_{10}.
For (c), both 201210_3 and 1362_7 are equivalent to 534_{10}.
For (d), both 1222_3 and 104_7 are equivalent to 53_{10}.

STARLOG 2000 & 2100

1. Perform the indicated operation. The exponents are in base 10 for clarity and to avoid subscripting an exponent.

(a) 10100111_2
    $+ \ 1110111_2$
    100011110_2

(b) 1100110011_2
    $+ \ 1111000011_2$
    11011110110_2

(c) 10111101_2
    $- \ 1001101_2$
    1110000_2

(d) 10010000_2
    $- \ 110011_2$
    1011101_2

(e) 10001000_2
    $- \ 1111111_2$
    1001_2

(f) 100111001_2
    $- \ 100010011_2$
    100110_2

(g) 10111_2
    $\times \ 1010_2$
    11100110_2

(h) 1101011_2
    $\times \ 1111_2$
    11001000101_2

(i) $(11011_2)^3$ =   **$\underline{100110011100011_2}$**

(j) $(1000_2)^4$ =   **$\underline{1000000000000_2}$**

(k) $(111000010_2) \div (110_2)$ =   **$\underline{1001011_2}$**

(l) $(11111100_2) \div (1001_2)$ =   **$\underline{11100_2}$**

Refer to Starlogs 2000 & 2100 answer keys.

For (d), the "borrowing" is a little tricky and is shown in two steps.

$$
\begin{array}{r}
0\ 1\ 1\ 1\ 10 \\
100\cancel{10000}_2 \\
-\quad 110011_2 \\
\end{array}
$$

$$
\begin{array}{r}
0\ 1\ 1\ 10 \\
\cancel{0}\ 1\ 1\ 1\ 10 \\
\cancel{10010000}_2 \\
-\quad 110011_2 \\
\end{array}
$$

Above and Beyond

2. Convert each of the following binary fractions to a bimal (same as a decimal except the base is 2).

(a) $\left(\dfrac{1}{11}\right)_2 = $ $\underline{\mathbf{0.01}_2}$

(b) $\left(\dfrac{111}{11100}\right)_2 = $ $\underline{\mathbf{0.01}_2}$

(c) $\left(\dfrac{11}{111}\right)_2 = $ $\underline{\mathbf{0.011}_2}$

(d) $\left(\dfrac{10101}{10101000}\right)_2 = $ $\underline{\mathbf{0.001}_2}$

(e) $\left(\dfrac{10}{101}\right)_2 = $ $\underline{\mathbf{0.0110011}_2}$

(f) $\left(\dfrac{1001}{11000}\right)_2 = $ $\underline{\mathbf{0.011}_2}$

A base 10 fraction is converted to a decimal by dividing the numerator by the denominator. Binary fractions are converted to bimals the same way.

3. **Without using base 10 as an intermediate step**, reduce the following binary fractions.

(a) $\left(\dfrac{10010}{100100}\right)_2 = \left(\dfrac{1}{10}\right)_2$

(b) $\left(\dfrac{11000}{100000}\right)_2 = \left(\dfrac{11}{100}\right)_2$

(c) $\left(\dfrac{11}{10010}\right)_2 = \left(\dfrac{1}{110}\right)_2$

(d) $\left(\dfrac{111}{100011}\right)_2 = \left(\dfrac{1}{101}\right)_2$

(e) $\left(\dfrac{1010}{1111}\right)_2 = \left(\dfrac{10}{11}\right)_2$

(f) $\left(\dfrac{1100}{100000}\right)_2 = \left(\dfrac{11}{1000}\right)_2$

Space Traveler's Training Manual Answer Key

For each problem, the <u>greatest common factor</u> (GCF) of the numerator and denominator is found and given below.

For (a), the GCF is 10010_2.
For (b), the GCF is 1000_2.
For (c), the GCF is 11_2.
For (d), the GCF is 111_2.
For (e), the GCF is 101_2.
For (f), the GCF is 100_2.

How is the GCF found without using base 10 as an intermediate step?

For (a), write the binary fraction horizontally and divide the numerator and denominator simultaneously by 10010_2 as shown below.

$$1_2 \; / \quad 10_2$$
$$10010_2 \;\overline{) \; 10010_2 \; / 100100_2}$$

The quotients 1_2 and 10_2, respectively, are the numerator and denominator of the fraction in lowest terms since 1 is the only divisor of both quotients.

It appears fractions in any base can be reduced by simultaneously dividing until 1 is the only divisor of both quotients. The resultant quotients, respectively, are the numerator and denominator of the fraction in lowest terms.

The previous solution is the most direct. Other solutions that are not as direct are possible. Here is an example:

For (a), suppose the only divisor recognized initially is 10_2? The simultaneous division would have been as follows:

$$1001_2 / \quad 10010_2$$
$$10_2 \;\overline{) 10010_2 / \; 100100_2}$$

Can the quotients be divisible by another number? Yes. Both quotients are divisible by 1001_2, so divide both quotients by 1001_2 as follows:

$$
\begin{array}{r}
1_2 / \qquad 10_2 \\
\hline
10010_2 \overline{)\ 1001_2 /\ \ 10010_2} \\
10_2 \overline{)100010_2 /\ 100100_2}
\end{array}
$$

What if the divisor is not so easy to find? For (e), the GCF of 1010_2 and 1111_2 is not obvious (unless, of course, base 10 is used an intermediate step).

Since the GCF can only be as large as the smallest number, the only possible divisors are between 1_2 and 1010_2. Since 1010_2 is even and 1111_2 is odd, the divisor cannot be an even number. Therefore, the only possible divisors are 11_2, 101_2, 111_2, 1001_2. The division is not shown here, but the only number that divides both 1010_2 and 1111_2 is 101_2.

4. **Without using base 10 as an intermediate step**, perform the indicated operations expressing each answer as a binary fraction in lowest terms.

(a) $\left(\dfrac{11}{1000}\right)_2 \times \left(\dfrac{100}{101}\right)_2 = \dfrac{11}{100 \cdot 10} \times \dfrac{100}{101} = \dfrac{11}{10} \times \dfrac{1}{101} = \left(\dfrac{11}{1010}\right)_2$

(b) $\left(\dfrac{1}{11}\right)_2 \times \left(\dfrac{110}{111}\right)_2 = \dfrac{1}{11} \times \dfrac{11 \cdot 10}{111} = \dfrac{1}{1} \times \dfrac{10}{111} = \left(\dfrac{10}{111}\right)_2$

(c) $\left(\dfrac{11}{1011}\right)_2 \times \left(\dfrac{10110}{1001}\right)_2 = \dfrac{11}{1011} \times \dfrac{1011 \cdot 10}{11 \cdot 11} = \dfrac{1}{1} \times \dfrac{10}{11} = \left(\dfrac{10}{11}\right)_2$

(d) $\left(\dfrac{110}{111}\right)_2 \times \left(\dfrac{1110}{1111}\right)_2 = \dfrac{11 \cdot 10}{111} \times \dfrac{111 \cdot 10}{11 \cdot 101} = \dfrac{10}{1} \times \dfrac{10}{101} = \left(\dfrac{100}{101}\right)_2$

(e) $\left(\dfrac{101}{1110}\right)_2 \div \left(\dfrac{1111}{111}\right)_2 = \dfrac{101}{1110} \times \dfrac{111}{1111} = \dfrac{101}{111 \cdot 10} \times \dfrac{111}{101 \cdot 11} = \dfrac{1}{10} \times \dfrac{1}{11} = \left(\dfrac{1}{110}\right)_2$

(f) $\left(\dfrac{11}{100}\right)_2 \div \left(\dfrac{101}{1100}\right)_2 = \dfrac{11}{100} \times \dfrac{1100}{101} = \dfrac{11}{100} \times \dfrac{100 \cdot 11}{101} = \dfrac{11}{1} \times \dfrac{11}{101}$

$= \left(\dfrac{1001}{101}\right)$ or $\left(1\dfrac{100}{101}\right)_2$

(g) $\left(\dfrac{11}{100}\right)_2 + \left(\dfrac{11}{1000}\right)_2 = \dfrac{11 \cdot 10}{100 \cdot 10} + \dfrac{11}{1000} = \dfrac{110}{1000} + \dfrac{11}{1000} = \left(\dfrac{1001}{1000}\right)$ or $\left(1\dfrac{1}{1000}\right)_2$

(h) $\left(\dfrac{11}{101}\right)_2 + \left(\dfrac{100}{1111}\right)_2 = \dfrac{11 \cdot 11}{101 \cdot 11} + \dfrac{100}{1111} = \dfrac{1001}{1111} + \dfrac{100}{1111} = \left(\dfrac{1101}{1111}\right)_2$

(i) $\left(\dfrac{111}{10010}\right)_2 - \left(\dfrac{10}{1001}\right)_2 = \dfrac{111}{10010} - \dfrac{10 \cdot 10}{1001 \cdot 10} = \dfrac{111}{10010} - \dfrac{100}{10010} = \left(\dfrac{11}{10010}\right)_2$

(j) $\left(\dfrac{101}{1001}\right)_2 - \left(\dfrac{10}{111}\right)_2 = \dfrac{101 \cdot 111}{1001 \cdot 111} - \dfrac{10 \cdot 1001}{111 \cdot 1001} = \dfrac{100011}{111111} - \dfrac{10010}{111111} = \left(\dfrac{10001}{111111}\right)_2$

The dot indicates multiplication. In (a) through (f), the numerators and denominators may be factored in order to cancel. Students' answers for (a) through (f) may not be in lowest terms if they do not "cancel."

In (h), students might think the least common denominator is 101_2 x 1111_2, but they should determine that 101_2 divides 1111_2, which means 1111_2 is the least common denominator. Using 101_2 x 1111_2 as the common denominator requires reducing the final answer to lowest terms.

Since 1 is the only common factor of the denominators in (j), the least common denominator is their product 1001_2 x 111_2 = 1111111_2.

STARLOG 2200

1. Convert each of the following numbers to base 10.

   (a) $A55_{12}$ = **1505**$_{10}$ (b) $1C3_{15}$ = **408**$_{10}$

   (c) $2FG_{17}$ = **849**$_{10}$ (d) BED_{16} = **3053**$_{10}$

   (e) ABC_{14} = **2126**$_{10}$ (f) $H5D_{20}$ = **6913**$_{10}$

   (g) $8CA_{13}$ = **1518**$_{10}$ (h) $G35_{20}$ = **5838**$_{10}$

Refer to Starlog 1500 answer key. Change the base to the current base.

2. Using the repeated-division method, convert each of the following base 10 numbers to the base indicated. When necessary, use letters for additional symbols.

   (a) 213_{10} = **159**$_{12}$ (b) 389_{10} = **15F**$_{17}$

   (c) 615_{10} = **2B0**$_{15}$ (d) 555_{10} = **1CF**$_{18}$

   (e) 487_{10} = **2B6**$_{13}$ (f) 236_{10} = **1A5**$_{11}$

   (g) 2983_{10} = **793**$_{20}$ (h) 400_{10} = **121**$_{19}$

Refer to Starlog 2200 answer key.

3. Make the multiplication table for base 12.

x	1	2	3	4	5	6	7	8	9	A	B	10
1	1	2	3	4	5	6	7	8	9	A	B	10
2		4	6	8	A	10	12	14	16	18	1A	20
3			9	10	13	16	19	20	23	26	29	30
4				14	18	20	24	28	30	34	38	40
5					21	26	2B	34	39	42	47	50
6						30	36	40	46	50	56	60
7							41	48	53	5A	65	70
8								54	60	68	74	80
9									69	76	83	90
A										84	92	A0
B											A1	B0
10												100

Refer to Starlog 2200 answer key.

STARLOG 2300 & 2400

1. Perform the indicated operation **using binary as an intermediate step**.

(a)
$$113_4 = \quad\quad 1 \;\; 01 \;\; 11_2$$
$$\underline{\times\;\; 22_4 = \quad\quad \times\;\; 10 \;\; 10_2}$$
$$3212_4 = \quad 11 \;\; 10 \;\; 01 \;\; 10_2$$

(b)
$$1223_4 = \quad\quad 1 \;\; 10 \;\; 10 \;\; 11_2$$
$$\underline{\times\;\; 33_4 = \quad\quad \times \quad 11 \;\; 11_2}$$
$$121011_4 = 1 \;\; 10 \;\; 01 \;\; 00 \;\; 01 \;\; 01_2$$

(c)
$$153_8 = \quad\quad 1 \;\; 101 \;\; 111_2$$
$$\underline{\times\;\; 17_8 = \quad\quad \times \quad 1 \;\; 111_2}$$
$$3105_8 = \quad 11 \;\; 001 \;\; 000 \;\; 101_2$$

(d)
$$27_8 = \quad\quad 10 \;\; 111_2$$
$$\underline{\times\;\; 12_8 = \quad \times \quad 1 \;\; 010_2}$$
$$346_8 = \quad 11 \;\; 100 \;\; 110_2$$

(e) $(13002_4) \div (12_4) = \mathbf{1023_4}$

$$\begin{array}{r} 1 \quad 00 \quad 10 \quad 11_2 \\ \hline 1 \quad 10_2 \,)\, 1 \quad 11 \quad 00 \quad 00 \quad 10_2 \end{array}$$

(f) $(3330_4) \div (21_4) = \underline{\mathbf{130_4}}$

$$\begin{array}{r} 1 \quad 11 \quad 00_2 \\ \hline 10 \quad 01_2 \,)\, 11 \quad 11 \quad 11 \quad 00_2 \end{array}$$

(g) $(702_8) \div (6_8) = \underline{\mathbf{113_8}}$

$$\begin{array}{r} 1 \quad 001 \quad 011_2 \\ \hline 110_2 \,)\, 111 \quad 000 \quad 010_2 \end{array}$$

(h) $(6631_8) \div (73_8) = \underline{\mathbf{73_8}}$

$$\begin{array}{r} 111 \quad 011_2 \\ \hline 111 \quad 011_2 \,)\, 110 \quad 110 \quad 011 \quad 001_2 \end{array}$$

Convert the symbols in base 4 to their binary equivalents as shown.

base 4 symbol:	0_4	1_4	2_4	3_4
binary equivalent:	00_2	01_2	10_2	11_2

Convert the symbols in base 8 to their binary equivalents as shown.

base 8 symbol:	0_8	1_8	2_8	3_8	4_8	5_8	6_8	7_8
binary equivalent:	000_2	001_2	010_2	011_2	100_2	101_2	110_2	111_2

2. Find the sum or difference in the base indicated. **Do not convert to base 10 before adding or subtracting.**

(a)
$$8B5_{16}$$
$$+\ A7C_{16}$$
$$\mathbf{1331_{16}}$$

(b)
$$479C_{16}$$
$$+\ 8ED_{16}$$
$$\mathbf{5089_{16}}$$

(c)
$$FAD_{16}$$
$$+\ CAB_{16}$$
$$\mathbf{1C58_{16}}$$

(d)
$$ABC_{14}$$
$$+\ 754_{14}$$
$$\mathbf{1432_{14}}$$

(e)
$$BDE_{17}$$
$$+\ 3GF_{17}$$
$$\mathbf{EDC_{17}}$$

(f)
$$D5H_{20}$$
$$+\ IDC_{20}$$
$$\mathbf{1CJ9_{20}}$$

(g)
$$1321_{16}$$
$$-\ A7C_{16}$$
$$\mathbf{8A5_{16}}$$

(h)
$$FAB_{16}$$
$$-\ CAD_{16}$$
$$\mathbf{2FE_{16}}$$

(i)
$$3B95_{16}$$
$$-\ 6CF_{16}$$
$$\mathbf{34C6_{16}}$$

Refer to Starlogs 2300 & 2400 answer keys.

Above and Beyond

3. Convert each of the following numbers to the base indicated **without using base 10 as an intermediate step.**

(a) 31323_4 = **$37B_{16}$** (b) 213011_4 = **$9C5_{16}$**

(c) $C6E_{16}$ = **301232_4** (d) FC_{16} = **3330_4**

(e) 21221_3 = **257_9** (f) 112201_3 = **481_9**

(g) 586_9 = **122220_3** (h) 148_9 = **11122_3**

Since 16 is the _second power_ of 4, _two-digit_ numbers in base 4 are equivalent to the hexadecimal symbols. The equivalents are shown below.

$00_4 = 0_{16}$	$10_4 = 4_{16}$	$20_4 = 8_{16}$	$30_4 = C_{16}$
$01_4 = 1_{16}$	$11_4 = 5_{16}$	$21_4 = 9_{16}$	$31_4 = D_{16}$
$02_4 = 2_{16}$	$12_4 = 6_{16}$	$22_4 = A_{16}$	$32_4 = E_{16}$
$03_4 = 3_{16}$	$13_4 = 7_{16}$	$23_4 = B_{16}$	$33_4 = F_{16}$

Since 9 is the _second power_ of 3, _two-digit_ numbers in base 3 are equivalent to the base 9 symbols. The equivalents are shown below.

$00_3 = 0_9$	$10_3 = 3_9$	$20_3 = 6_9$
$01_3 = 1_9$	$11_3 = 4_9$	$21_3 = 7_9$
$02_3 = 2_9$	$12_3 = 5_9$	$22_3 = 8_9$

Space Traveler's Training Manual Answer Key

STARLOG 2500

1. Make the multiplication table for base 7.

x	1	2	3	4	5	6	10
1	1	2	3	4	5	6	10
2		4	6	11	13	15	20
3			12	15	21	24	30
4				22	26	33	40
5					34	42	50
6						51	60
10							100

Refer to Starlog 2200 answer key.

2. Find the products.

(a) 542_6
$\times\ 34_6$
$\mathbf{32552_6}$

(b) 44.44_6
$\times\ 35.2_6$
$\mathbf{3035.252_6}$

(c) 503.4_6
$\times\ .234_6$
$\mathbf{221.5324_6}$

3. Find the quotients to two hexamal places **without using base 10 as an intermediate step.**

(a) $(4212_6) \div (0.5_6)$ = **$\underline{5124.45_6}$**

(b) $(5334_6) \div (12_6)$ = **$\underline{411.13_6}$**

(c) $(4.325_6) \div (1.4_6)$ = **$\underline{2.43_6}$**

For problems 1 and 2, refer to Starlog 2500 answer key. Hexamal placement is the same as decimal placement.

Space Traveler's Training Manual Answer Key

Above and Beyond

4. Convert each of the following base 6 fractions to a hexamal (same as a decimal except the base is 6).

(a) $\left(\dfrac{3}{4}\right)_6$ = **0.43_6**

(b) $\left(\dfrac{13}{14}\right)_6$ = **$0.5\overline{2}_6$**

(c) $\left(\dfrac{1}{2}\right)_6$ = **0.3_6**

(d) $\left(\dfrac{3}{5}\right)_6$ = **$0.\overline{3}_6$**

Base 6 fractions are converted to hexamals in the same manner as base 10 fractions are converted to decimals by dividing the numerator by the denominator.

5. State the divisibility rules for 2, 3, 4, and 5 in base 6.

In base 6, a number is divisible by 2 (even number) if and only if the <u>units digit is 0, 2, or 4</u>.

In base 6, a number is divisible by 3 if and only if the <u>units digit is 0 or 3</u>.

In base 6, a number is divisible by 4 if and only if the number is even (the number ends in 0, 2, or 4) <u>*and* dividing the number by 2 yields an even quotient</u> (the quotient ends in 0, 2, or 4).

In base 6, a number is divisible by 5 if and only if the <u>sum of the digits is 5 or a number divisible by 5</u>.

Fractions are easier when these divisibility rules are applied.

6. Convert each of the following hexamals to a base 6 fraction **in lowest terms**.

(a) 21.003_6 $= \left(21\dfrac{3}{1000}\right)_6 = \left(21\dfrac{3 \div 3}{1000 \div 3}\right)_6$
(mixed)

$= \left(21\dfrac{1}{200}\right)_6 = \left(\dfrac{4201}{200}\right)_6$
(mixed) (improper)

(b) 521.014_6 $= \left(521\dfrac{14}{1000}\right)_6 = \left(521\dfrac{14 \div 2}{1000 \div 2}\right)_6$
(mixed) (mixed)

$= \left(521\dfrac{5}{300}\right)_6 = \left(\dfrac{240305}{300}\right)_6$
(mixed) (improper)

(c) 0.504_6 $= \left(\dfrac{504}{1000}\right)_6 = \left(\dfrac{504 \div 12}{1000 \div 12}\right)_6 = \left(\dfrac{35}{43}\right)_6$

(d) 521.014_6 $= \left(\dfrac{24453}{10000000}\right)_6 = \left(\dfrac{24453 \div 3}{10000000 \div 3}\right)_6$

$= \left(\dfrac{5335}{2000000}\right)_6$

Converting hexamals to fractions is exactly the same as converting decimals to fractions, except the base is 6. Apply the divisibility rules from the previous problem to determine the GCF of the numerator and denominator.

For (c), the GCF of 12_6 is not obvious. Actually, the numerator and denominator were divided by 2 three times as follows:

$$\left(\frac{504 \div 2}{1000 \div 2}\right)_6 = \left(\frac{232 \div 2}{300 \div 2}\right)_6 = \left(\frac{114 \div 2}{130 \div 2}\right)_6 = \left(\frac{35}{43}\right)_6$$

which is dividing by $(2^3)_6 = 12_6$

7. **Without using base 10 as an intermediate step**, perform the indicated operations expressing each answer as a base 6 fraction **in lowest terms**.

(a) $\left(\dfrac{3}{12}\right)_6 \times \left(\dfrac{4}{5}\right)_6 = \dfrac{3}{4\cdot 2} \times \dfrac{4}{5} = \dfrac{3}{2} \times \dfrac{1}{5} = \left(\dfrac{3}{14}\right)_6$

(b) $\left(\dfrac{1}{3}\right)_6 \times \left(\dfrac{10}{11}\right)_6 = \dfrac{1}{3} \times \dfrac{3\cdot 2}{11} = \dfrac{1}{1} \times \dfrac{2}{11} = \left(\dfrac{2}{11}\right)_6$

(c) $\left(\dfrac{5}{100}\right)_6 \times \left(\dfrac{200}{23}\right)_6 = \dfrac{5}{100} \times \dfrac{100\cdot 2}{5\cdot 3} = \dfrac{1}{1} \times \dfrac{2}{3} = \left(\dfrac{2}{3}\right)_6$

(d) $\left(\dfrac{10}{55}\right)_6 \times \left(\dfrac{41}{13}\right)_6 = \dfrac{3\cdot 2}{5\cdot 11} \times \dfrac{5\cdot 5}{3\cdot 3} = \dfrac{2}{11} \times \dfrac{5}{3} = \left(\dfrac{14}{33}\right)_6$

(e) $\left(\dfrac{3}{5}\right)_6 \div \left(\dfrac{20}{23}\right)_6 = \dfrac{3}{5} \times \dfrac{23}{20} = \dfrac{3}{5} \times \dfrac{5\cdot 3}{3\cdot 4} = \dfrac{1}{1} \times \dfrac{3}{4} = \left(\dfrac{3}{4}\right)_6$

(f) $\left(\dfrac{4}{11}\right)_6 \div \left(\dfrac{20}{11}\right)_6 = \dfrac{4}{11} \times \dfrac{11}{20} = \dfrac{4}{11} \times \dfrac{11}{4\cdot 3} = \dfrac{1}{1} \times \dfrac{1}{3} = \left(\dfrac{1}{3}\right)_6$

(g) $\left(\dfrac{3}{4}\right)_6 + \left(\dfrac{3}{12}\right)_6 = \dfrac{3\cdot 2}{4\cdot 2} + \dfrac{3}{12} = \dfrac{10}{12} + \dfrac{3}{12} = \left(\dfrac{13}{12}\right)$ or $\left(1\dfrac{1}{12}\right)_6$

(h) $\left(\dfrac{3}{5}\right)_6 + \left(\dfrac{4}{23}\right)_6 = \dfrac{3\cdot 3}{5\cdot 3} + \dfrac{4}{23} = \dfrac{13}{23} + \dfrac{4}{23} = \left(\dfrac{21}{23}\right)_6$

(i) $\left(\dfrac{11}{30}\right)_6 - \left(\dfrac{2}{13}\right)_6 = \dfrac{11\cdot 3}{30\cdot 3} - \dfrac{2\cdot 10}{13\cdot 10} = \dfrac{33}{130} - \dfrac{20}{130} = \dfrac{13}{130} = \dfrac{13}{13\cdot 10} = \left(\dfrac{1}{10}\right)_6$

(j) $\left(\dfrac{5}{13}\right)_6 - \left(\dfrac{2}{11}\right)_6 = \dfrac{5\cdot 11}{13\cdot 11} - \dfrac{2\cdot 13}{11\cdot 13} = \dfrac{55}{143} - \dfrac{30}{143} = \left(\dfrac{25}{143}\right)_6$

For (i), the least common denominator (LCD) is not obvious. Is there a smaller common denominator than 30_6 x 13_6? A similar problem in base 10 might shed light on this problem.

The LCD for the base 10 denominators 18 and 24 is not too obvious. The LCD can be found easily by dividing the denominators simultaneously as shown below.

$$6\overline{)\begin{array}{cc}3 & 4 \\ 18 & 24\end{array}}$$

or

$$\begin{array}{c}2\overline{)\begin{array}{cc}3\overline{)\begin{array}{cc}3 & 4 \\ 9 & 12\end{array}} \\ 18 \quad 24\end{array}}\end{array}$$

The LCD is 6 x 3 x 4 = 72, <u>the product of the divisor(s) and the final quotients</u>. To rename the fractions with the LCD as the new denominator, <u>multiply the numerator and denominator by the final quotient of the other denominator</u>. The denominator 18 is multiplied by *4*, and the denominator 24 is multiplied by *3*.

Note: For the denominators 18 and 24, the GCF is obviously 6, but more than one division may be needed for less-obvious problems. The multiple division given above shows that the LCD will be found regardless of the number of divisions.

Use the previously described method on (i) as follows:

$$3_6\overline{)\begin{array}{cc}10_6 & 3_6 \\ 30_6 & 13_6\end{array}} \qquad\qquad \textbf{LCD} = \textit{3}_6 \cdot \textit{10}_6 \cdot \textit{3}_6 = \textit{130}_6$$

Multiply 30_6 by 3_6 and multiply 13_6 by 10_6 to obtain the LCD of 130_6.

Acknowledgements

The authors would like to thank the people who gave us invaluable input and suggestions.

Asa Kleiman, coauthor of *It's Alive* and *It's Alive and Kicking*, made wonderful recommendations to sharpen the dialogue. In addition, Asa thought our Space Traveler should be worried about more than simply getting back home. Why not prove Earthlings are intelligent in order to save Earth from demolition? Terrific idea, Asa.

We were unsure of the extent of knowledge the teachers using this book would have of alternate number bases. Could the answer be understood by elementary and junior high teachers who knew little or nothing about other number bases? Jeri Hitchcock, a former elementary teacher, helped us answer that question by reading through the answer key. Jeri, thanks so much for giving of your valuable time.

Our editor, Libby Lindsey, spent countless hours tackling the vast maze of numbers. This kind of math book can become a burden at times, but her professionalism and attention to detail helped us make it through as smoothly as possible. Thank you, Libby.

Finally, we would like to thank our families for their patience and support. No one could be more excited than they are about the completion of this project.

About the Authors

Nick Bollow is an eighth grader at Marshfield Junior High School. In competition with more than 4,000 talented Wisconsin students, he attained first place on the ACT. Bollow enjoys mathematics greatly and was enthusiastic about cowriting this book. Although Nick says working with two teachers was enlightening, he's still not sure what "outasight" and "far out" really mean.

Rita Berg earned a B.S.E. in mathematics from Arkansas State University in 1980 and a M.S. in statistics from the University of Arkansas in 1982. After working as a statistician for several years, she taught math and statistics part-time for several universities while raising her son and daughter. She currently teaches high school mathematics in Marshfield, WI, and she loves singing as much as she loves math.

Marya Washington Tyler is the author of three best-selling books for gifted and talented students, *Real Life Math Mysteries*, *It's Alive*, and *It's Alive and Kicking*. She has taught gifted and talented students in Marshfield, WI, for 10 years and has four gifted children of her own. She dreams of vagabonding around the world, but has no plans for space travel at this time.

The authors of *Alien Math* welcome your questions, comments, or suggestions. You may e-mail them at alienmath@hotmail.com.

Other math titles from Prufrock Press:

• It's Alive!

Mary Ford Washington, Asa Kleiman,
& David Washington
ISBN 1-882664-27-2, $14.95 paperback

It's Alive! is a book of weird, crazy, and bizarre math problems guaranteed to challenge, stimulate, and gross-out math students everywhere. In addition to making math highly motivational, this book focuses on teaching students to translate real-life problems and questions into mathematical equations. All the problems are based on known facts. Students learn math, science, and a little trivia at the same time! This is math the way it ought to be-tough, fun, and a little weird! **Grades 3-9**

• It's Alive … And Kicking!

Mary Ford Washington, Asa Kleiman,
& David Washington
ISBN 1-882664-30-2, $14.95 paperback

It's Alive …and Kicking is another book of weird, crazy, and bizarre math problems guaranteed to challenge, stimulate, and gross-out math students everywhere. In addition to making math highly motivational, this book focuses on teaching students to translate real-life problems and questions into mathematical equations. This is math the way it ought to be—tough, fun, and a little weird! **Grades 3-9**

• Extreme Math

Marya Washington Tyler & Kip Tyler
ISBN 1-882664-96-5, $19.95 paperback

Kayakers, skydivers, bronco riders, adventure racers, and many more are the subjects of this exciting math book. Imagine your students tackling math word problems drawn from the extreme sports of polar ice swimming, scuba diving, or even mountain climbing. In *Extreme Math*, students discover the excitement of using their mathematics problem-solving skills to answer actual questions faced by extreme sports athletes. **Grades 4-12**

• Real Life Math Mysteries

Marya Washington Tyler
ISBN 1-882664-14-0, $19.95 paperback

Drawn from interviews with working people in professions ranging from zookeeper to horse stable owner, the problems in this book stimulate student interest. Not only will students learn to formulate equations from word problems, but they will also see firsthand the power of math in the real world. With the activities in this book, your students will solve mathematics dilemmas faced by a technician at a recycling center, a doctor at a children's clinic, an announcer at a radio station, and many more. Each activity is presented in the words of the professional who faced the dilemma. **Grades 3-12**

• Chances Are

Nancy Pfenning
ISBN 1-882664-35-3, $24.95 paperback

From helping to win a card game, to projecting the rate of growth of a virus, the uses of probability and statistics are virtually endless. This book offers an excellent enhancement to statistics and probability. For teachers of elementary students, the book offers simple, hands-on lessons and activities about probability and basic statistics. For teachers of older students, advanced statistical concepts are discussed and activities are provided. **Grades 3-12**

• Developing Mathematical Talent

Susan Assouline & Ann Lupkowski-Shoplik
ISBN 1-882664-92-2, $27.95 paperback

Written for teachers and parents of mathematically talented youth in elementary and middle school, this book provides a means for identifying the needs of mathematically talented students and matching both school and home experiences to those needs. The book describes a systematic model for programming and planning for mathematically talented youth. It provides teachers and parents with the tools they need to plan effectively for their students. **All Levels**

PRUFROCK PRESS INC.™

Visit our website at http://www.prufrock.com for our complete listing of math titles and to request your free catalog.

Camp Fraction
Solving Exciting Word Problems Using Fractions
Set around a trip to summer camp, students work with fractions in a problem-solving format, while learning a little history, trivia, and fun facts about a number of different items.
Grades 4–6 $11.95

Creative Writing
Using Fairy Tales to Enrich Writing Skills
Use fairy tales to challenge and motivate your students. This activity book contains fun reading and writing activities that pique students' interest in creative writing.
Grades 4–8 $11.95

Extra! Extra!
Advanced Reading and Writing Activities for Language Arts
The book includes standards-based independent language arts activities for students in grades K–2 such as developing a newspaper and inventing new words.
Grades K-2 $11.95

Math Problem Solvers
Using Word Problems to Enhance Mathematical Problem Solving Skills
The standards-based problem solving strategies addressed in this book include drawing a picture, looking for a pattern, guessing and checking, acting it out, making a table or list, and working backwards.
Grades 2–3 $11.95

Puzzled by Math!
Using Puzzles to Teach Math Skills
Puzzled by Math! offers a collection of mathematical equations, knowledge, and skills in puzzle form. Standards-based content addresses addition, subtraction, multiplication, division, fractions, decimals, and algebra. Thirty-five exciting and challenging puzzles are included, as well as suggestions for using the material for a classroom learning center.
Grades 3–7 $11.95

Survival on the Reef
Exploring Amazing Animals and the Ways They Adapt to Their Environment
This challenging activity book addresses many essential skills and knowledge contained in the National Science Teachers Association standards using activities focused on the exciting environment of a coral reef, its inhabitants, and the ways these inhabitants have adapted to their world.
Grades 2–3 $11.95

Writing Stretchers
15 Minute Activities to Enrich Writing Skills
Standards-based activities address the areas of reading, writing, vocabulary, content literacy, creativity, and thinking skills, giving students a chance to enrich their writing skills.
Grades 4–8 $11.95

For a complete listing of titles in this series, please visit our website at

http://www.prufrock.com

PRUFROCK
PRESS INC.